From Autistic to Awesome

09/12
To Jeff,
Best Wishes!
God bless you and your family.
Sincerely,

FROM
AUTISTIC
---------------- TO ----------------
AWESOME

A Journey of Spiritual Growth through
Life with My Special-Needs Child

Paul M. Powell

APR
AIRPORT RHODE PUBLISHERS
ATLANTA, GA

This is a true story; however, some of the names and other details have been fictionalized. This book is inspirational and informational only. No content in this book should be used as a substitute for seeking medical, mental health or other professional advice.

FROM AUTISTIC TO AWESOME. Copyright © 2012, by Paul M. Powell.

For information, address Airport Rhode Publishers LLC, 35 Patterson Road #465989, Lawrenceville, GA 30044.
www.autistictoawesome.com
Author email: paul@autistictoawesome.com

Printed in the United States of America.

All rights reserved. No part of this book may be reproduced in any form by any electronic or mechanical means including photocopying, recording, or information storage and retrieval without permission in writing from the author.

Cover by: Cicero Clamor

Library of Congress Control Number: 2012912822

ISBN: 978-0-615-67076-8

First printing, August 2012

10 9 8 7 6 5 4 3 2 1

*To my son Matthew, my daughter Jaida,
and my wife Sonya.*

*To John Sr., Mary, Theresa, Clarence, and Rosetta.
You provide an irreplaceable foundation of love and
support for our family.*

*To the parents, children, families, friends, and caregivers
of persons affected by autism and other disabilities; yet
determined to be a light in this world.*

Contents

Prologue iii

Chapter One
DEVELOPMENTAL DELAYS *1*

Chapter Two
DAYCARE DILEMMAS *17*

Chapter Three
INTERVENTION *27*

Chapter Four
DIAGNOSIS *49*

Chapter Five
NOT BY SIGHT *55*

Chapter Six
MOURNING IN MARRIAGE *67*

Chapter Seven
SEARCHING FOR A CURE *79*

Chapter Eight
MADE USEFUL *111*

Chapter Nine
GOD USES PEOPLE *123*

Chapter Ten
FINDING PEACE *149*

Chapter Eleven
HERE COMES THE SON *175*

Chapter Twelve
LESSONS LEARNED *185*

Epilogue 193

Acknowledgements 197

Prologue

"WHY?" "WHY," I thought to myself, as I knelt before God, "are you allowing this to happen?" I found myself crying out, "Why, God, why? My son is just a defenseless little boy. He's just a boy!" The questions did not find a permanent home in my heart, but they definitely reared their heads amid an occasional flood of tears. Though I was afraid to overstep my boundaries with the God who made everything, I could not help but ask.

I wrote From Autistic to Awesome: A Journey of Spiritual Growth through Life with My Special-Needs Child for anyone who can relate to that sentiment. While meant to be a source of help, I did not write it as a how-to or a data-driven guide only providing facts and figures to educate the reader about autism. I meant to write a shared account from one affected parent's heart to another's about the twists and turns of life that come with having a special-needs child—specifically one with an autism spectrum disorder.

Like most parents with special-needs children, my wife, Sonya, and I dearly love our son. We think he is the most handsome and wonderful boy in the world, and we would do anything for him. Through him, we have come to know the path of significantly changed plans and dreams. We know what it is like to wake up morning after morning and go through a special routine, often rigorous and emotional, just to get out the door. We know what it is like to hear friends and family talk about potty training and realize, with all of our child's developmental delays, we forgot going to the bathroom independently was even on our list of goals.

We also know what it feels like to be at the park, doing our best to ensure our child stays safe, only to look up, and notice another parent managing a child who seems old enough to be speaking, but is not. Instead, the child is spinning around in circles, indifferent to the other children on the playground or just unable to keep up physically with them. At that moment, though we would never wish autism or developmental challenges on any other family, we feel a momentary sense of comfort and encouragement from the reminder that we are not alone—someone else knows what it feels like, and they are going through it too.

This book is a "we know what it's like" story for other loved ones of autistic children who just want to know that someone, somewhere, can relate to what they are going through. My wife and I have found that most parents we have met who have autistic children really needed only two things in great measures—real resources to help their child (ren) get well and knowing there are others out there who understand exactly what they are going through.

As awareness of autism grows, more and more books about it crop up, covering everything from healing remedies to behavioral therapy to educational planning. Even books like this one, focused on the personal account of one family, have been making an appearance. I wondered if there were room out there for another manuscript on this subject, and, if I could contribute something meaningful to the discussions already in progress. My answer was yes. There is room for another unique account about a little boy with autism and his family. Hopefully, it will find its way into the hands of a parent, grandparent, friend, sibling or caregiver who wants to know there is hope. No matter how hard things seem today, others can attest from experience that it is enough to love our children and to continue to dream for them.

Finally, I have found raising a child who has autism to be transformative in every area of my life, most notably my Christian faith—and so I address that throughout the chapters of this book. In some parts of From Autistic to Awesome: A Journey of Spiritual Growth through Life with My Special-Needs Child, I talk in passing about my faith. In other sections, I discuss it more directly, while doing my best to avoid language that might be considered by some as exclusive to religious circles. I believe my story can benefit anyone traveling a similar path, who, through the trials of a life affected by autism, winds up on the road to a greater personal faith.

Chapter One

DEVELOPMENTAL DELAYS

IT WAS OCTOBER 2004. Matthew had been with us for almost a year. He was beautiful, and my wife and I would sometimes just sit together on the edge of our bed and gaze at him. Nine months had passed since he came home from Benton Howard Davis hospital, and the hardships it took for him to come into the world no longer dominated our thoughts.

Sonya had endured an illness known as Hyperemesis gravidarum during her pregnancy. She had morning sickness in which the nausea and vomiting normally associated with pregnancy did not cease at the end of the twelfth week. Sonya suffered for many weeks with dehydration, weight loss, and the emotional trauma resulting from the risk of losing Matthew. She was on bed rest at home for seven weeks receiving intravenous fluids. At one point, she required trips to the hospital every other day for monitoring. In Sonya's thirty-first week of pregnancy, we rushed her to the hospital in the middle of the night because she had preeclampsia. The doctors delivered Matthew that morning at a weight of two pounds and six ounces, and he spent six weeks in the hospital's neonatal intensive care unit (NICU).

It was a difficult time, but it was behind us now. We were once again able to dream about who our son might be someday. Sonya and I derived so much joy from having a child that it amazed me to think God allows all people everywhere to experience it. The Bible verse stating "He causes his sun to rise on the evil and the good, and sends rain on the righteous and the unrighteous" (Matthew 5:45 NIV) came alive for me in a way I had never before understood.

I daydreamed back to the start of our life together before Matthew. Like many other couples with an autistic child, autism entered our world after a storybook start to our marriage—one in which our dreamy expectations of married life were confronted with few challenges. Sonya and I met in our late twenties while members of the same church, which, at that time, was the focus of our social life. In 1991, Sonya had graduated from Spelman College in Atlanta with a degree in mathematics. Following her studies, she moved back to her home state of Alabama to assist in our church's outreach efforts there, while working as a high school teacher. Five years later, Sonya moved to New Jersey where for a time, she worked in women's ministry as a full-time staff member in our church. Sonya was bright and outgoing, and she had a reputation as a determined leader who genuinely cared about the well-being of others. During the years that she lived in New Jersey, she and I met and began dating.

Approximately five years from our first date, on an April morning in 2002, Sonya and I were married before a congregation of five hundred friends and family in a beautiful church in Wyckoff, New Jersey. Eight months earlier, Sonya survived the 9/11 attack on the New York City World Trade Center buildings where she worked at that time. Many of our friends thought that was why I asked her to marry me, but the truth was I loved her—and she loved me.

Throughout a picture-perfect, six-month engagement, we felt God's blessing on our lives and our decision to be married. Our friends and family were constantly surprising us with gifts in the form of money, presents, celebrations, and words of encouragement. It was humbling to receive so much love and support.

Our wedding morning was unseasonably cold for April in New Jersey, with a light snow coming down. It made the day seem like one of a kind. I could not have imagined a better wedding day or a better woman to be marrying than Sonya. She was beautiful, thoughtful, and supportive, and, most importantly to me, she was a loving person. We reflected on the fact that this day, which we had prayed about for so long, had come.

The following morning, on a warm, fair afternoon, Sonya and I arrived at our honeymoon spot—Puerto Vallarta, Mexico. We stayed at a beautiful resort that sat on the shore of the Pacific Ocean. Our new life together was on its way. Every day seemed easy and the nights were filled with stars. Conflicts were nonexistent, and, we had no fear any would come.

We believed our post-honeymoon feelings were the norm for married life. We spent a year enjoying each other before getting pregnant in the following spring, and our life was so good that it felt surreal. At the time, it was nearly impossible to imagine anything could ever change. However, that was two years earlier, and though we had much to be thankful for, life was different with a prematurely born baby.

HIGH RISK FOLLOW-UP

EARLIER IN THE summer, Sonya scheduled a home visit with an organization called Babies Can't Wait. She found out about them through a social worker at the hospital where Matthew was born. Babies Can't Wait is a state-administered, federally funded program, which was established under the Individuals with Disabilities Education Act (IDEA). They assisted families by providing services to enhance the development of children between birth and three years of age. One of those services, which we needed, was developmental evaluations for high-risk babies. Sonya contacted them once Matthew became old enough to be seen. If Babies Can't Wait found delays, they then assisted in obtaining occupational, speech, or other required therapy or interventions.

The Babies Can't Wait evaluators arrived at our home on a sweltering, July afternoon. I was at work, and Sonya was at the apartment to meet them. When I got home that evening, Sonya was cheerful about the visit, and she described it as a bright spot in her day. Sonya found the evaluators to be friendly, great with Matthew, and knowledgeable. They began the evaluation by inquiring about Matthew's behavior and motor skills, such as: did he make bubbles with his lips or respond to our voices and facial expressions. Following the questions, they performed an examination of Matthew, which Sonya said looked more like play than it did anything else. They gave him toys to see what he would do with them and made silly faces to see if, and how, he responded.

The Babies Can't Wait staff was pleased to let us know Matthew was doing fine and did not qualify for any of their services. We were appreciative because we knew, even before he was born, all the stress he underwent in the womb put Matthew at risk for slow progress in his abilities, as well as other general health issues. The visit eased our minds, and, for the remainder of the summer, our prayers transitioned from appeals for help to expressions of gratitude.

Similar to the feedback from the Babies Can't Wait evaluation, older women friends of ours made us smile when they saw Matthew and declared that he was going to be an early walker or talker. These women were mothers who had raised and cared for many children in their day—some of them had even raised their grandchildren. We considered them authoritative voices on the subject of children, and we sat up straight and paid attention when they spoke. "Oh, he's going to be on his feet and walking early," they would say with a nodding gesture of seniority and adding, "I can tell," with a winked eye, which made their proclamations seem unquestionable. Their assertions of Matthew's promise gave us a much-needed jolt of optimism at a time when we did not see any sign that Matthew would be walking or talking anytime soon.

We were not worried, but we were praying for some indication Matthew might be "exceptional and above the preemie crowd." I had to admit, somewhere deep down inside, I wanted to see something remarkable from Matthew in order to feel, beyond a doubt, as if his premature arrival, low birth weight, and NICU stay really were behind us.

CELEBRATING ONE YEAR

SONYA ASSURED ME I was looking a little too deep into the matter and having a party for Matthew would be fine. She reminded me of what a victory it was that Matthew was here and healthy, which was something she believed was worth the biggest celebration we could throw. For much of my adult life, I had questioned why people put on lavish birthday parties in honor of little children who were barely aware of what was happening. Therefore, as Sonya and I sat down to plan, I had reservations. I saw images of barbeques, hired clowns, face painters, and all the family and friends a backyard could hold, starting as a children's event and ending up as a party-hearty scene with grown-ups at the helm. However, as I listened and considered what she was saying, I realized Sonya was right. We needed to celebrate Matthew's birthday—in a child appropriate manner, of course.

Matthew's birthday was on the twenty-third, and the get-together turned out to be a very heartwarming event. We invited family and friends, most of whom had infants and toddlers themselves. Halfway through the event, Matthew fell asleep in his little rocker in front of the television. The other children continued to play around him—everyone had a great time.

The one-year-old mark was significant to us because, from that point on, Matthew's growth would reveal more about his development than it did the previous twelve months. Going forward, missed milestones would be much more obvious. Walking and talking in his first year would have been signs he was developmentally on target, but not walking and talking in his second year would sound alarm bells, as it could be evidence there might be something amiss.

In the months following his first birthday, we took Matthew for a one-year development check. Benton Howard Davis Hospital had their own high-risk clinic that followed up with the progress of preemie children born there. The feedback on Matthew's progress was excellent. We were surprised to see how well he was doing compared to the other preemies his age. He was healthy and responsive to us. He was alert, attentive, regularly looked into our eyes with connectedness, and giggled at our funny, facial expressions. He and Sonya had bonded. Several parents, who were also waiting to have their children evaluated, asked how old Matthew was and were surprised at how well he was progressing.

The visit to the clinic was eye opening because, even though we had been told Matthew might experience delays, we had not comprehended what that meant practically. Going to the clinic and seeing other prematurely born children provided us a glimpse of what early childhood delays looked like. For the first time, we were able to see what it might look like if Matthew were a stage or two behind normal, infant progress.

We left the clinic feeling grateful on one hand and a little shaken up on the other to have seen firsthand the uphill battle Matthew had escaped. From what we could tell, our baby boy was a shining example of a typical and healthy child; the doctor at Benton Howard Davis Hospital agreed.

GOOD-BYE TO AVERAGE DEVELOPMENT

OUR APARTMENT IN West Orange, NJ was the place where our life together began, but in February 2005, the lease was up, and we decided not to stay for a third year. Our downstairs neighbors had changed, and our surroundings were not as amiable as they had been previously. It was time to move on. We deliberated over the idea of leaving New Jersey and moving to Georgia, but we needed time to think it through. Sonya missed the South, and she wanted to go home to be closer to her family, but I was not sure how I felt about going so far away from the region where I had spent so much of my life. To give ourselves more time to plan, we stayed in New Jersey for the time being, but moved to Maplewood, which was a four-square-mile suburban town less than ten minutes south of West Orange.

Unlike our West Orange apartment, the two-story, red brick building we moved into had little, if any, character. There were about twenty units, all without any special amenities or distinct architectural features. The appeal of the cramped, two-bedroom dwelling to us was that another young, newly married couple we knew from church also lived there. They were warmhearted, deeply spiritual people. The wife, who was from the South, and Sonya had become close. We trusted, and shared the same moral values, with this couple. It meant a lot to us to live in close proximity to them.

We settled into Maplewood. And, over the next few months, we continued to discuss the possibility of moving to Georgia and researched its housing market. At that time, the real estate prices in the country were at the peak of what many experts were calling a "bubble" of inflated prices. It was nothing short of astounding to me to discover if we relocated to Georgia, we could afford a home on one salary. Gradually, I became more comfortable with the idea of uprooting us from the New York metropolitan area. I was not yet ready to pick up and go, but we were discussing it frequently, and the thought was settling in.

Once we were moved in, our new home turned out to be cozy. We were keeping a simple schedule, and we were dedicated to maintaining our new tradition, which was family time. In the evenings, we played lullabies for Matthew on his compact disc player and sang the songs he loved. One evening, following dinner, I stepped out of our bedroom and happened upon one of those precious, infant moments we were relishing so much at the time. Sonya was on the couch, and Matthew was sitting on her lap, listening as she sang to him. Whenever she paused from singing, he would pull himself up to her face, give her a kiss on the cheek, and then look expectantly into her eyes for more songs. After each kiss, Sonya obliged Matthew, and I was content watching as their mother-to-baby exchange continued.

Matthew was so happy and alert that, unlike the previous months, we now felt confident he was at the doorstep of talking. It was a far cry from what we had seen with him back in the fall. He was sixteen months old, and all the pieces of the puzzle were in place. In fact, Sonya and I were already being careful about what we verbalized in Matthew's presence, preparing for when he would start repeating our every word. Before we got pregnant, we used to discuss all the things we thought we needed to do in order to be the best possible influence on our children; to us, saying only uplifting statements was an important part of that.

We saw other indications as well, that Matthew would be talking soon. His crib was in the bedroom next to ours. It was a white, wooden bed with animal motifs on the bedding. Sometimes, after sleeping in his crib, Matthew would wake up crying and looking around for us. On many of those occasions, he would call, "Da-da, Da-da," until I came and picked him up. When he mimicked our expressions and appropriately put his tiny fingers on parts of his body in response to questions; such as, "Where is your nose?" or "Where are your ears?" we just knew we had a little genius on our hands. Our belief that our child had unlimited potential was reinforced week after week by his actions and growth. Matthew's progress was exactly as we had hoped it would be. A few months later, the summer brought change—literally and geographically. It had been over a year since Sonya and I had begun our talks about moving to Georgia, and it had been three or four months since we made the decision to actually do it. But, finding a job in Georgia was not proving to be an easy task. I applied for a large number of positions and requested referrals from people I knew who had contacts in the Atlanta area, but nothing was panning out. We realized it could take some time for me to land a job.

Now that we were resolved about relocating, I was eager to move on to the next phase of our life. Nevertheless, I also felt we needed to allow enough time for me to find a position and ensure as secure a transition as possible. Sonya wanted to make a wise move as well, but she was torn by feelings of detachment from the life we had known in New Jersey before having Matthew. She longed to be closer to her family. In addition to wanting a new start as a family, her most important relationships were in the South.

More than anything else, I felt that we needed to pray more about the situation. I believed, if God had put it on our hearts to move to Georgia, he would open a door to enable us to do it.

Therefore, one evening after a conversation with Sonya, I prayed: believing God would take care of things as He had always done. Within one day, I was able to come home from work and let Sonya know that we could move right away.

A few weeks earlier, I had confided to a co-worker that I desired to move my family to Georgia. That conversation led to an opportunity to speak with someone who could authorize me to keep my current role with the company, but work remotely from Georgia. Apparently, because I had a favorable reputation, I could just take my laptop and go. As a part of the arrangement, I agreed to travel back to the New Jersey office once a month, which I was more than happy to do. Not only did it ensure my office relationships stayed strong, but it also enabled me to visit my family. I saw it as God's perfect way of meeting Sonya's need to move soon, our family's need to move with financial confidence, and my need to transition from family and friends in a manner I could handle. We thanked God.

We decided we would live with Sonya's mother, Theresa, in a suburb of Atlanta for a three-month period. Our goal was to forego an apartment right away in order to save and buy a house sooner. In less than a week from getting the approval from my company, we hired a moving company to transport our belongings to Georgia. They took everything that could be squeezed into their truck, and we threw out, gave away, or stored the few remaining items.

On July 16, we drove our packed car sixteen hours to Riverdale, Georgia. It was a predominantly, African-

American suburb south of Atlanta. Sonya's mother lived alone in a four-bedroom house in a subdivision of about sixty homes. This would be our home for the next three months, and it was our third home in the past six months. I found it interesting that I was moving to the Southeast in search of a better life for my family, when, just a generation earlier, my parents trekked north from that region for the very same reason.

The four months we spent in the tiny town of Maplewood would turn out to be a significant and cherished period of our early life with Matthew. This was not because we did anything so spectacular while there, in fact, our life at that time was commonplace; rather, it was because a commonplace life would become a thing of the past for our family as Matthew grew, and developmental delays began to appear. Our months in Maplewood were the last time we would clearly remember Matthew at age-appropriate development.

THE SHOCK OF OUR LIVES

GEORGIA WAS THE beginning of a completely new chapter of our life. As the months went by, every aspect of our life changed rapidly and dramatically predicated on one simple fact—we began to have a growing suspicion that something was wrong with our son. Even though his delays came to light over a period of more than eight or nine months, the emotional impact of what was happening made it seem sudden, as if there were a very immediate, distinct, and clear-cut change in Matthew. The tiny personality we had been nurturing for some time seemed to fade.

Matthew had just started walking and independently feeding himself. We were sure this was a little later than what was considered average. Additionally, for some inexplicable reason, he was no longer calling me "Da-da" when he woke up crying, and he did not add any new words. We were not sure exactly how many words he should have been saying at the time, but it became apparent he was lagging behind in his speech development. His first Babies Can't Wait evaluation showed he was on track and required no early intervention, but that was a year behind us. Matthew brought a tremendous amount of joy into our life, and we were nowhere near panicking, but our excitement to hear him speak more words had now shifted to a budding concern and suspicion that something serious was going on. Matthew was now twenty months old.

Moving to the South changed our lifestyle because we were no longer among the church community and friends we knew so well in New Jersey. As a couple, we reached out to build new relationships at church in Atlanta, but we were the most isolated we had been since getting married. Working from home fulltime was great in a multitude of ways, but it made us even less communal.

Being together so much was a wonderful time for the three of us because it offered stability at a time when there were so many new components to our life. However, it also meant we were not often around other families with toddlers. We had little with which to compare Matthew's behavior. We spent extended time with few parents. Therefore, it was not apparent to most people that Matthew was falling behind developmentally because they did not know him well enough to assume his exact age. They usually assumed that he was younger than his actual age.

Matthew had stopped showing much interest in the people around him; rather, he fixated on whatever he wanted. He was not attempting to do things independently and did not seem to be able to focus on any one task for more than a moment. Wrestling away from hugs and disengaging in play involving action and reaction—such as, peekaboo or rolling a ball back and forth—were now prevalent. We began to observe Matthew more closely, desperately hoping what we thought we were seeing was not really happening.

One of our most eye-opening experiences took place one weekend morning at church. Prior to arriving in Atlanta, Sonya and I already knew we would join an affiliate congregation to our church in New Jersey. Sonya was already familiar with this congregation from years earlier when she was in college.

The teachings and most of the practices of the Atlanta church were identical to our church in New Jersey; including a strong emphasis on the children's ministry, which was important to us. It was pretty commonplace for any member who was able to participate in the Sunday programs for children to do so, whether it was teaching, assisting, or setting up classes. Soon after joining, Sonya and I volunteered to teach for a few months.

We co-led a two-and three-year-old class with another married couple. We enjoyed that age group and thought it would be easier for us to manage our Sunday morning schedule if we taught the same class in which Matthew participated. On most Sundays, the class had anywhere from ten to twelve children. The night before our first class, we reviewed the lesson plan given to us, and we took the liberty of editing it. We were sure that some of the activities listed were too advanced for that age group, and we wondered who put the plan together. We were shocked and puzzled by how far off was their assessment of the capabilities of children that age.

During class the next morning, we went through an awakening of sorts regarding Matthew's development. We were stunned as, one by one, the children who were Matthew's age arrived to class communicating in sentences, following directions, and carrying out various tasks independently. They were not running around the room in pursuit of every colorful object that caught their eye. We could not believe what we were seeing.

We realized we did not need to edit the lesson plan at all. We had prepared for the class using Matthew as our point of reference, but we were way off. What we were witnessing was made even clearer when the time came for the children to sit on the carpet in a group to watch a video. All of them were well behaved, orderly, and quiet as they intently gazed at the animation on the screen. This scene appeared almost surreal from my perspective, and, among it all, in high contrast, was Matthew, who was spinning, rolling back and forth, and twisting his body away from myself and Sonya as if his life depended on getting away from us. Even the other children stared at him, glancing back to my wife and me, as if to ask, "What is happening with him?" or "Why did we bring a baby to our class?"

After the video, we carried out our responsibilities as planned for the remaining thirty minutes. All of the children, including Matthew, had a great time, but I was silently distraught and nearly tempted to panic. As well, I was worried about Sonya. During the class, there was no time to talk about what we, along with everyone else, were observing. I knew Sonya, and if I were feeling crestfallen, more than likely she was too. When class ended, we dutifully signed out each child as their parent came to pick them up, and we cleaned the room—deliberately not speaking to each other as it was next to impossible to talk about anything besides what was going on with Matthew.

On our way out, I picked up Matthew, and the three of us crossed the street to the parking lot in the same "loud" silence. When we got into the car and settled Matthew in his seat, I was the first to muster a word. My hands shook, and my thoughts were unclear. Feeling overwhelmed and fighting not to let my voice sound worried or sad, I quietly pushed words out,

"Did you notice how different Matthew was from all the other kids? I was blown away. I didn't realize."

"Yeah. It was definitely eye-opening," Sonya replied.

"He's like a little baby compared to the other kids. I wonder if he's catching on slower because he's with us so much instead of in daycare or something like that. Once we figure out where we're living, maybe we should put him somewhere during the day so he can be with other little kids."

"That's probably part of it, but we do need to go ahead and get him evaluated too so that we know what's going on and can get whatever type of help he needs."

"Since he's been born we just haven't been around that many kids his age. I didn't realize all the stuff he should be able to do. These kids were talking."

"I know, but we have to remember everything Matthew went through and the time he spent in NICU and everything else."

"Yeah." I agreed.

"How did you feel when you saw that?" This was the one question I was hoping Sonya would not ask me and the reason why I was hesitant to start talking.

"It took everything I had to not start crying," I replied.

"Me too," she replied.

It was now apparent to us that our thirty-one-week premature baby, who seemed to defy the odds since we brought him home almost two years earlier and had been doing so well, might not escape the stumbling blocks faced by the other early-born children treated at the Benton Howard Davis Early Intervention Clinic. Matthew's well-being meant the world to us and was our top priority, but, during a quiet moment when we had time to consider what might be happening, we also realized, as parents, we might not be exempt from the same fear and uncertainty those other children's parents were enduring. Momentarily, we wished we still lived in New Jersey because Benton Howard Davis Hospital specialized in infant and toddler development. But, we were not in New Jersey, and we needed to get help regardless.

Chapter Two

DAYCARE DILEMMAS

SEPTEMBER WAS PASSING by, and I was surprised at the daily, continually changing weather pattern of hot, high-temperature, sunny afternoons and a regular, thick downpour of rain in Riverdale. Sometimes, the flip-flop in conditions shifted from afternoon to evening on the same day. Sonya and I liked the area, but it had been two months since we arrived in Georgia, and we were still praying to find a house and move into it by October. As a result, we spent a lot of time viewing houses online and in person. It was a good way for me to become familiar with the different cities and towns in the metro-Atlanta area.

Before leaving New Jersey, Sonya had met with Matthew's pediatrician to find out what needed to be done regarding his routine care and to ensure his progress was on track. The doctor advised, since Matthew had been born prematurely, it was critical to monitor a number of different aspects of his health. In addition to identifying a proper pediatrician for Matthew, she instructed us to request referrals for other specialists, including: an ophthalmologist and a cardiologist. She also advised us to schedule periodic visits with Babies Can't Wait. My wife came out of the meeting with a pertinent to-do list of what was needed to make sure Matthew was receiving the proper care.

Friends of ours in Atlanta, whose children were older,

recommended a local pediatrician, so Sonya made an appointment. As a first course of action, we intended to get Matthew checked out as soon as possible.

October was close and, after many weeks of driving all over town to see homes, we finally located a house forty-five minutes southwest of Atlanta and thirty minutes east of the Alabama state line. It was a four-bedroom, cottage-style home. Sonya liked it a lot. We put in a bid, and our offer was accepted. The closing date was set for October 10, and we would move in by October 16. It was almost three months to the day since we arrived in Georgia, and exactly the timing we had been praying for. God continually built my faith in the way that He worked things out for us. I had no doubt that, as we prayed and sought help, He would work on Matthew's behalf in the same way.

Matthew's second birthday was coming up within a week. He was no less a source of joy and wonder to us, but he had still not said a word other than "Da-da," and we had not heard that since we resided in Maplewood. Also, he was small for his age and lacked balance when he walked. One of the main characteristics we started to notice that concerned us was he wandered off with no regard for where Sonya or I were, even when we called his name. Every now and then, he stopped and turned at the sound of our voices, but, more often than not, his feet carried him nonstop toward whatever his eyes saw until we intercepted him. He seemed almost oblivious to our presence.

Now that we had moved into our own home, we wanted to find a local daycare for Matthew, as we had planned. However, we were worried Matthew might not be able to handle the activities in a daycare environment. He could not stop moving and could not focus his attention for longer than a few seconds at a time. We wondered if he would be better off in a daycare environment with children who were younger than he was. On the other hand, we did not think he was so far behind that he could not become accustomed to a setting with children his own age, and we wondered if being among more developed children for a time would help him along. Since we really did not know, we thought the best thing to do was to take Matthew with us to see pre-K schools and let those teachers meet him and give us some direction.

After researching several schools, Sonya made preliminary visits to see their facilities and find out what their requirements were to accept children. In the meantime, a neighbor on our block gave us the name of a preschool, Fresh Meadows, which we decided to check out. It was less than ten minutes from our house, which was convenient for us, so we hoped it would be a good place for Matthew. Our neighbor enrolled her daughter there, and she had spoken highly of the school.

Sonya was surprised to learn that every one of the schools she contacted had a ten-to-one child-to-teacher ratio. We could not imagine any teacher keeping up with Matthew while working with nine other children at the same time. He was not mature enough to follow directions independently. He also had no awareness of danger. At home, we had toddler gates in a number of doorways because he could easily run to a staircase and fall down due to a lack of perception of what was coming when he stepped off the top step. Since the ten-to-one ratio was what the state of Georgia allowed, I considered I might be unaware of classroom techniques that enabled one teacher to attend to ten two-year-olds, but I was concerned Matthew would be unsafe in such a setting; on the other hand, I wanted him to have the daily exposure to other children.

Sonya was excited and I was tentative when we stepped into Fresh Meadows with Matthew. Upon pulling into the parking lot, we were immediately impressed by the facility. It was a one-story, brick building, about the size of a large house, sitting on half an acre of land. It was very well maintained, and there was a playground out back with modern-looking, bright-colored play sets for the children. The polished green, red, and yellow structures looked new. On one side of the building was an in ground pool, which was suitably sized for toddlers. I liked what I saw, but remained skeptical, Even as we were entering the building, Matthew was trying to run off.

Once inside, we saw rooms to the left and right of the entrance. Aluminum-framed glass doors separated the rooms from the hallway. Further toward the back of the hall where we were standing, there were five or six other rooms with identical doors, each labeled with a name designating an age group, such as "Turtle Twos" or "Sprouting Fours." To me, it felt more like a childcare factory than the warm and loving pre-K environment I had imagined. Immediately before us was a front desk attended by a woman who seemed preoccupied with administrative work. She barely looked at us or greeted us with sincerity; I wondered why. We approached the desk and Sonya let her know who we were, why we were there, and that she had spoken with the school's director.

The woman did not introduce herself, but politely said she would get the appropriate person to speak with us. As she was getting up out of her chair, a petite, blonde woman in her early thirties appeared from around the hall corner. She looked pregnant enough to deliver at any moment, and she approached us like a burst of sunshine with a southern drawl. She reminded me of an animated personality, like that of a children's television show host, and she was the extreme opposite of the woman sitting behind the front desk.

"Hiiiiii…how are you? I'm Charlotte Downsby. I'm a lead teacher at Fresh Meadows."

"Hi, I'm Sonya Powell"

"Paul Powell," I said, "and this is our son Matthew."

"Oh he's precious. Ya'll are a real nice-looking family. Yes sir, a real nice-looking family."

My wife continued, "We are thinking about having our son come here and thought we would stop by to see the school."

"Well, we hope you will choose Fresh Meadows." Ms. Downsby said, as I continued to hold Matthew's hand so he would not run off down the hall.

"He will take off if I let him go," I said, as Matthew twisted his whole body to break free and pursue the construction paper flowers on the wall.

"Oh, he's fine," Ms. Downsby said.

Then she walked us through the room where Matthew would be if we chose Fresh Meadows, introduced us to the teachers for the two- and three-year-olds, and fielded our many questions. Our biggest concern, which we stressed four or five different times, was we were not sure if Matthew was mature enough to be in a class with the other two-year-olds. We shared with her what we had seen in our Sunday school class. Ms. Downsby assured us Matthew would be fine once he was away from us more often and in a more social environment. She told us she saw it all the time. We were encouraged because we desperately needed to hear something even remotely indicating Matthew would soon be fine—whether we believed it or not.

Sonya and I drove out of the Fresh Meadows parking lot interpreting our reservations as possibly something we just needed to get over in order to take the next step forward in Matthew's life. We thought seriously about how unaware we were of his delays just a few weeks earlier, and we accepted the fact that we were not yet fully informed about what was best for him. We believed it was our responsibility to learn all we could and to figure out what was best as we went forward. We entertained the possibility that the teachers at Fresh Meadows might know more than us about Matthew's ability to attend their school and to grow from being there. It was Thursday when we visited, and, on Monday morning of the following week, we would drop off Matthew for the day.

Monday came fast, and we drove Matthew to daycare together and returned home. Although we were eager to pick him up in the afternoon to find out how the day went, we felt far more comfortable with him being at Fresh Meadows than we thought we would be. We had a feeling that we were doing the right thing, and our son was with professionals who would care for him and the other children without developmental delays whom he could imitate. We felt good about it.

When Sonya picked up Matthew later that afternoon, the teacher told her Matthew cried most of the day, and she had to hold him a lot. This was not much different from how he was at home, so we assumed he was just getting used to his new environment. On his daily report provided to us by the school, the comments section contained statements such as: "Matthew was uncooperative and would not listen or follow directions." We were shocked there was no more insight into his behavior other than to state he was uncooperative. Considering the conversation we had with Ms. Downsby, we found the notes to be discouraging and insensitive, and we spent the evening contemplating whether we made the right decision to send Matthew to Fresh Meadows. Maybe the classes were too big.

Was it a bit premature to take him out of Fresh Meadows after one day? We were so very new to pre-K and daycare. Should we do more due diligence before making any changes? Despite our reservations, we decided to let him attend the next day. We dropped Matthew off on Tuesday morning, and I could not stop thinking about him and wondering if he was OK. Would the teachers get frustrated with him and mistreat him because he could not keep up? Was he enjoying the experience, or was he sad and out of place?

I realized I needed to talk through my feelings to get beyond them, and I wondered how much of what I was feeling was just me going through my own adjustment to trust someone, other than Sonya, with our child. I did not want to worry Sonya, so I called my mother. She had worked in a pre-K school for over thirty years and was qualified to give feedback about what I was thinking and feeling. I dialed her number in New Jersey, and she picked up.

"Hey, how are you?"

"Good. How are you," she replied.

"I'm ok, but I wanted to ask you something."

"What is it?"

"Well, I'm not sure if I'm just acting weird or what I should think about the nursery school we have Matthew in."

"What do you mean?"

"I don't know. I almost feel like I don't know if I should have him there."

"Does the school allow you to show up and look in on him?"

"Yeah."

"Well maybe you can do that."

"I probably will," I said, even though I was not completely sure that I wanted to do that.

"You don't sound too comfortable with the school."

"I don't know that I am."

"Well that's not unusual."

My interest was piqued, "Really?"

"Yes. People start their kids here and take them back out the next day all the time. If they're not sure, they don't play around."

The feeling that I was a clingy, over-protective father began to lessen. I felt a little more confident knowing others had done what I was considering.

"I can see why," I said.

"Oh yes, I have seen it many times. Are you going to take Matthew out of there?"

"I don't know yet. We'll see."

THE DILEMMA

WHEN I PICKED Matthew up on Tuesday, the room was eerily quiet as I entered and spoke to Matthew, who was playing with a toy animal near a bookshelf. The other children in the room stared at me with the same concerned look I had seen on the faces of the children in our Sunday school class. According to the lead teacher, Matthew cried less than the day before but she still had to hold him at times. His daily report contained similar comments indicating he was uncooperative and disobedient. The only positive thing she could find to say was that he ate a lot of pasta at lunch. I sensed there were things she was holding back, so I asked her frankly and cordially if she felt Matthew could handle being there. She said that she felt, as is the case with some children, Matthew needed more time to mature.

I thanked her, took Matthew, and left. When I told Sonya what had happened, we agreed to take Matthew out of Fresh Meadows. I was angry the school was not forthcoming after his first day. I wondered how, and if, they planned to communicate to us about Matthew, other than writing bad behavior remarks about him on his daily report.

On one hand, I felt Fresh Meadows could have spent more time with us when we visited the school and could have been better equipped to provide professional feedback on whether or not Matthew could handle their classroom environment. On the other hand, looking beyond my anger and defensiveness, I was hurt because I felt a daycare center had rejected my son. Although I should have focused my concern solely on Matthew, I felt embarrassed that he was not able to function well at the school.

I thought about how children, especially boys, who have learning and development challenges, are incorrectly diagnosed, and labeled as "behavioral problems." In the school system where I grew up I had personally witnessed poor and minority boys placed in special education programs and tagged as the "bad kids." It seemed strange to me, even as a child, that the special education classes were mostly comprised of disadvantaged children. Students and teachers viewed the minority children not placed in those classes as exceptions. As an adult, I came to understand some of the reasons behind it, such as unprepared and improperly trained teachers or an inflexible and ill-equipped school system. I determined I would never allow my child to suffer from that type of labeling. I did not believe any child should—no matter what their race or social position.

The sea of emotions I was experiencing left me anxious, confused, and wondering what the next step to help Matthew should be. We could not believe the answer was to just wait and hope he would get better; though, I was tempted to do just that. It was hard to understand how anything good could come from what was happening in our life, and my feelings toward God were wavering between "I still trust you and know everything will be fine," and "God, why are you not helping us?" At the time, I had no idea how often I would wrestle with these kinds of feelings before even scratching the surface of what it meant to trust God fully with the son He gave me.

Chapter Three

INTERVENTION

Though the fig tree does not bud and there are no grapes on the vines, though the olive crop fails and the fields produce no food, though there are no sheep in the pen and no cattle in the stalls, yet I will rejoice in the LORD, I will be joyful in God my Savior.
- Habakkuk 3:16-18
(NIV)

MATTHEW SMILED AND giggled delightfully with his legs stretched out in front of him, while sitting on our living room carpet. It had been well over a year since we heard him even attempt to speak a word, and, though we were praying and believing he would talk, we were living with the reality that it was possible we might never hear audible words from him again. But, for the moment, Matthew was engaged in a toy activity box Sonya and I had picked up for him. It was eight-inches high with different toddler exercises on either side. Bright orange, red, and blue rollercoaster-shaped wire frames were on the top. Wooden beads were threaded through the wires so they could slide along the wire's curves. Matthew was enthralled with how smoothly he could maneuver the beads up one side of the wire and then watch them free fall down the other. Each time he let a bead drop, his giggling got louder. As usual, I was enjoying the sight of him happy at play.

As Matthew continued to grip the wooden balls and slide them up one side of the wire arc, and then release them down the other, I began to play along by enunciating the words "up" and "down" in sync with his movement of the beads. Matthew found my words amusing, and he chuckled even harder than at first. "Uuuuuup, dowwwn," I said, intentionally drawing out my words in an effort to prompt him to laugh again. "Uuuuuuup, dowwwn." By now, Sonya had turned her attention away from the television show she was watching, and she began to take in our little exchange. Within a few minutes of trading words for laughter, Matthew became even more interested in our game. And, all of a sudden, as if out of nowhere, he decided to join in with my voice. As clear as day, he repeated my words, "Uuuuuuup, dowwwn. Uuuuuuup, dowwwn." Sonya and I looked at each other in astonishment as if to say, "See there, we knew it would happen."

We were certain this was the spark that was going to light his communication capabilities on fire. We were so exhilarated that we did not know what to do with ourselves. Words could not describe the relief we felt from what we saw as a clear indication Matthew could and would talk. His voice was like a precious song to our ears, and, to make sure we were not dreaming, we continued repeating the words in order to hear him say them back to us. I said, "Uuuuup," and he said, "Uuuuup." I said, "Dowwwn," and Matthew said, "Dowwwn." Sonya and I were both smiling from ear to ear, and we felt like we had just won the lottery. I looked at my wife and said, "We're on our way." She nodded in agreement. Matthew's achievement brought an enormous sense of promise into our home, and, for a time, displaced our temptation to worry about the future.

MORE CHILDREN, OR NOT

THERE WAS A lot of change going on in our life in the early part of 2006, and yet, in the mysterious and unspeakable way people begin to yearn for children of their own, the longing to have another child gradually emerged within me. It was an unburdened and pleasant thought accompanied by imagery of Matthew bonding with a little brother or sister. Nevertheless, I was careful not to assume Sonya would feel the same. She had suffered a difficult pregnancy, and it was her life that had been endangered. I wanted to be sensitive to how she might be feeling and careful not to reopen a wound that may not yet have completely healed. At the same time, I considered the possibility Sonya would find healing by having another child who, prayerfully, would not have autism.

I was uncertain how to bring up the subject. Concerned she might be distraught by the very thought of caring for another child while raising Matthew, I knew the timing of the discussion would be critical to good communication, so, I brought it up at a time when we both were usually pretty relaxed—during a family getaway.

It was nearing five o'clock in the evening, and we were driving through one of the more populated stretches of highway in Montgomery, Alabama. Our car trailed a partially hidden sun that appeared to dart in and out among a dense layer of clouds. We gained an extra hour by driving southwest out of Georgia and crossing from Eastern Standard Time into Central Standard Time. There were plenty of other cars on the road, and traffic was moving about five miles faster than the 65 mile per hour speed limit. Behind our backs, Matthew slept peacefully in his car seat. The topic of another baby fit right in with the discussion we were already having about where we wanted to see our family in the upcoming years, nevertheless I wanted to ease into talk of a baby in order to get a sense of how comfortable Sonya might be with the idea.

Continuing to feel hesitant, I spoke quietly, "I know this might be a stretch, considering what our life is like now with Matthew and all that we've been through, but I still find myself thinking about giving him a brother or sister."

"Me too." I paused for a second, making sure I had correctly heard what Sonya said.

"Really?" I was prepared to explain why I felt the way I did, but I was caught off guard because no explanation was needed.

"Yeah. I don't want him to be alone. There needs to be somebody, besides you and me, who has a long-term relationship with him." I was amazed we were having this conversation so easily because, for so many months prior, with all that was going on, it was not unusual for us to have trouble communicating on issues related to big decisions. "The only thing I wonder is - what are the chances you could have another pregnancy as bad as the first one?"

"I don't know," she replied, "but we can check with the doctor and find out. Everything I have ever heard is that women who have severe and prolonged morning sickness once are likely to have it again. I read an article about a woman who had four children, and, with every pregnancy, she was really sick. When the interviewer asked her why she went through it over and over, she just said that she wanted to have children."

We sat quietly for a moment. I was not sure what Sonya was thinking, and I needed to carefully select my words before speaking what was now going through my mind. "I wonder, what are the chances we could have another child with autism?" As I suspected, Sonya was thinking about the same thing, "That's God's business," she replied, "We'll love our children no matter what. I'm willing to take the chance."

I interpreted Sonya's courage as evidence of her recovery. It helped me to believe she was OK, yet I remained concerned and did not want to push her. "Maybe we could pray about it, try for a period of time, and if we don't get pregnant, then just move on. We can always adopt later on if we want to. There are a lot of children who need homes." I felt the need to tell her what else was going on in my mind. "I didn't know what you would think. The last thing I remember you saying was that you never wanted to go through pregnancy again."

"There was a time when I did feel that way. I think I needed to be sure I was past that. I'm in a different place now, so we should try."

We talked and laughed, envisioning Matthew running around with a sibling. The notion brought a smile to our faces.

After talking more, we proceeded to make a plan that any doctor would have laughed at. Although it could obviously take much longer to get pregnant, we decided to try to conceive for a period of three or four months and then move on. I guess it did sound unrealistic in light of all the people in the world who spent years trying to have a baby—some without ever succeeding. Nonetheless, it was March, and by the time the summer rolled around we wanted to have tried without getting anxious about it, and then move on with our life.

In our minds it was also a way of approaching things with open heartedness toward whatever direction God might take us. Just because we wanted something, did not necessarily mean it was best or was what God wanted for us. We were determined not to reach a place where we were driving ourselves crazy over something that was not meant to be. Our decision to pray and try for a set period of time may not have been the most practical plan in the world, but it was our way of letting go of it to God and maintaining our peace of mind. Sonya's doctor confirmed she was healthy enough to have another baby.

PURSUING MORE FOLLOW-UP

SONYA CONTACTED BABIES Can't Wait of Georgia

to try to schedule an in-home visit similar to the one Matthew had back up north. For whatever reason, she did not hear back from anyone at Babies Can't Wait right away. She assumed it was because of the large number of families they served. Her speculation was later confirmed during one of our first appointments with Matthew's new pediatrician, Dr. Mercer.

We did not expect Dr. Mercer to provide Matthew with the treatment he needed, but we assumed she could help us understand to what extent he was behind in his development, and tell us what steps we should take to help him get caught up. Dr. Mercer was able to help us get started on the latter

She advised us not to bother pursuing Babies Can't Wait; indeed, they were backed up. As far as she knew, it could take up to a month for them to respond. Dr. Mercer provided all of the other specialist referrals that Sonya requested. She believed, because Matthew was a preemie and a boy, he probably needed more time to catch up. She said, in her experience, boys took longer to develop socially than did girls, but, with time, he would probably be fine. We breathed a momentary sigh of relief and found hope in her assessment of Matthew—even though we weren't sure we agreed 100 percent.

Dr. Mercer gave us a referral for occupational therapy to Atlanta's Augustine National Children's Hospital. She was certain Matthew was delayed at present, and her approach to his situation was to take direct action— first, check his hearing to rule that out as the cause of his unresponsiveness and inability to pick up language, and then have Matthew start seeing a speech therapist.

The twice-a-week visits to Augustine National Children's Hospital were scheduled in the morning, and both Sonya and I went. This experience turned out to be surprisingly pleasant. The facility was well designed, and the immaculate grounds were landscaped with trees and flowers. It was a bit of a walk from the parking lot to the entrance, but someone driving a large passenger golf cart came to transport us to the door. Matthew loved the ride, and we loved the care that was being shown to us.

Inside, the main entrance was spotless, and the elevators to the third floor were easy to find. We went up and exited into a carpeted hall, which was colorfully decorated with a cheerful, children's motif. It exuded warmth and child friendliness. I felt as if the organization were saying "Your child will be safe and well taken care of here." We believed it.

Not only was it roomy, but the Child Therapy Services waiting room was also stocked with toys, books, and an overhead video monitor showing cartoons. Matthew's therapist was a young woman in her twenties with blonde hair, whose name was Katherine. She was professional, knowledgeable, and courteous, which meant a great deal to us as we entered a new life in which we relied heavily on medical and educational professionals. Good bedside manner and customer service were extremely important, and, though most providers that we saw were considerate and patient, a few were not. Given the fact that common, everyday tasks, such as going to the grocery store with Matthew were stressful, we did not need difficult appointments with healthcare professionals added to that list.

Matthew's evaluation at Augustine National Children's Hospital first led to addressing his speech needs; it also quickly revealed his need for help with fine and gross motor skills, as well as common tasks, such as: putting on his shoes and his awareness that these tasks needed to be done. We returned later to Dr. Mercer for the occupational therapy referral to address these sorts of deficiencies.

As Matthew completed his first couple of weeks of therapy, we learned a lot about him that we previously did not know; such as he was very tactile oriented. Simply put, he loved touch. Burying his fingers in dirt, sand or wood chips thrilled and soothed his brain. This explained why Matthew always chose to sit and run his fingertips through the moist, gritty soil at the playground rather than go down the slide with the other children.

It gave us confidence to see how Katherine managed Matthew and prepared him to focus on activities to help him grow. She deeply massaged his hands, feet, and legs. Also, she allowed Matthew to play in bins filled with rice, which, she explained, also provided input to his brain. We did not understand exactly how that worked, but we witnessed that it did work, so we did the same at home when Matthew was really wound up.

As we learned more about Matthew through occupational therapy, we were able to experiment with new ways to help him focus. Now, understanding things; like he was calmed by touch, helped us see that Matthew could progress through therapeutic methods. It also helped us not to feel helpless when he was overstimulated (which was often). Instead, we began to provide sensory input to him by immersing his hands in bags filled with popcorn kernels. We found that the kernels pressing against his nerve ends had an amazing effect on his ability to relax and maintain self-control. We looked forward to his weekly therapy sessions with Katherine because they gave us hope. However, this was just a piece of the puzzle for us; we still needed to know why Matthew's behavioral issues were occurring in the first place.

Our questions impelled us to read and research on our own. We started on the internet by pulling up search engines and looking up key words, such as: "developmental delays" or "early childhood development." We found it interesting that, somewhere in most of the articles and reports we viewed, something called "autism spectrum disorders" or "ASD" was mentioned. I was startled to read the comments posted by parents of autistic children because many of their stories about their own children mirrored our current experiences with Matthew.

In order to find out more, I went to our local library and checked out a stack of books on the subjects of early childhood development and autism. As Sonya and I continued to read, we were even more surprised to discover how many of the autistic traits described fit Matthew to a T. Sonya and I began to discuss the possibility Matthew had this ailment called "autism."

A week after reading a description of the symptoms and possible causes of autism, we concluded that whatever we were dealing with required a diagnosis—not the hunch of a husband-and-wife team. We knew we needed professional input to determine whether or not our suspicions were true. Although we did not disregard what we thought we were seeing, we tempered our inclination to jump to conclusions.

Also, we began to be confronted with the emotional side of what it would mean to move from believing Matthew was a slow starter with delays he could grow out of with a little help, to accepting the possibility he had some sort of permanent, neurological or biological disorder.

THE RESURGENCE OF WORDS

BABIES CAN'T WAIT eventually called Sonya back. When she answered the phone the conversation went just as we anticipated,

"Hello, may I speak to Sonya Powell please?"

" This is she."

"Hi this is Ms. Frank from Babies Can't Wait of Georgia. You left us a message regarding your son, Matthew Powell."

"Yes. I wanted to find out how we can get him evaluated and maybe get some early intervention help for him. He was born at thirty-one weeks and we think his speech and behavior are behind where they should be."

"Ok. What is his birth date?"

"October 23, 2003," Ms. Frank was still courteous, but she

paused for a second or two as she calculated, then continued, "So he will be three before the month is out?"

"Yes," replied my wife.

"We only provide services from birth to three years old, so by the time we schedule an appointment, he would no longer be eligible. Once children turn three, they become eligible for services through your county. All counties offer early intervention services through the public school system."

"So I would need to contact our county's school system?"

"Yes, and they could let you know details about what is offered and what is the process to receive services."

"Ok, thank you. I will give them a call."

"Ok, Goodbye."

"Goodbye."

Sonya contacted our county's administrative offices and was put in touch with the head of the public school system's early intervention special-needs program. They provided an overview of their services and their goal, which was to try to close the gap between a child's current skills and the ones required to participate in a kindergarten class. The process would begin with an evaluation of Matthew by the early intervention team at the school he would attend. A couple of weeks before Matthew's evaluation, he had another breakthrough that we considered worth celebrating.

Matthew was sitting near Sonya on the tiled floor in our breakfast area among a pile of his plastic cast toy animals. He loved animals more than anything else; he also loved seeing them in videos, books, and real life. As he played, he lined up the animal figures in a single file: first the horse, then the cow, then the hippo, and so on. Recently, we had noticed he did the same single-file formation with his pieces of sausage at breakfast and his peas at lunch, although we did not know why.

As Matthew worked intently on his make-believe circus train, Sonya attempted to engage him in conversation,

"Matthew, what is this?" she asked in a toddler friendly tone, while pointing to the zebra in his caravan. Matthew smiled as usual, looking as if he wanted to talk but was not able to. "This is a zeeebra," Sonya continued. Matthew smiled again without endeavoring to look in her direction. She continued, hoping to entice him with the same childlike voice, "Matthew," he did not look at her, "Matthew, this is a hor-see. Do you like the hor-see?" "Hor-see," Matthew replied unexpectedly. Sonya and I paused and looked at each other. With a huge smile on her face, she looked at him, "Yes Matthew, "Hor-see." Again, he repeated, "Hor-see."

This was the second word we heard him speak in over a year and it was like music to our ears.

SPECIAL EDUCATION

MATTHEW'S EVALUATION WAS held at River Pond Middle School. We met with three therapists and two special education teachers. Because we were meeting with people who were trained and worked with delayed children all the time, we were hopeful. Our expectation was that they would be something like an intense, think tank and would come up for air from their research to examine our son, tell us exactly what was happening, and advise what we could do to help him get better. The actual experience turned out to be somewhat different.

Sonya and I were given several questionnaires about Matthew's current behavior and abilities, as well as some general information about our family. While we were completing the forms, two of the evaluators took Matthew into an adjacent room with a large window through which we could see them. They performed several activities with Matthew. Most were play scenarios to see what decisions he would make and how he responded to different situations. Other activities were things like giving him a brush to see if he knew what to do with it. From what we could observe, he was having a good time. We were relieved because, for the moment, we were getting a break from continually keeping up with Matthew.

When the forms were completed and the evaluators working with Matthew were done, everyone came back to the table for a discussion. We were surprised the group was so formal. Though everyone was friendly, it felt more like an official proceeding than an early education evaluation. They made sure to read us our rights as parents and to ensure we understood we had the right to have others present. Our signatures acknowledged and documented that these things had been explained to us. A peculiar and uncomfortable silence came over the room at that point.

We were green to the workings of public school systems, but we later learned these were all components of creating Individualized Educational Plans (IEPs) for children. As we became better informed about public school requirements for IEPs, we understood the possibility for conflict between parents and schools was high and could easily end up in legal action by the parents against the schools. This group had probably been through some difficult sessions and was well versed on the protocol they needed to follow.

As they asked us questions we expounded on the fact that Matthew was a preemie who had spent a month and a half in the NICU. We described how he was starting to talk a little when we lived in New Jersey and how he used to touch his eyes, ears, and nose when prompted, which he was no longer doing. We were proud to tell them he could now say "horse,"— although he pronounced it in two syllables. We discussed his lack of attention and related how he ran off every chance he got.

Then, we asked if, based on what they saw and heard so far, they thought Matthew had autism or something similar. Quickly and courteously they clarified that their evaluation was for educational services planning only, and they did not conduct psychological evaluations or provide a diagnosis. The scope of the services provided by the special-needs program was solely focused on preparing Matthew to gain the skills he needed to enter kindergarten successfully at the appropriate time. They reiterated their primary concern was to close the gap between what he knew and what he needed to know for school.

Overall, the meeting went well. The only bump in the road was one of the therapists seemed to have slightly less interpersonal skills than Sonya and I would have liked. At the end of the meeting, the special-needs program director stated they would document their findings and list goals for Matthew to help him in the areas in which he was deficient. We set a date for a follow-up appointment in two weeks, at which time we would review their findings and recommendations and sign off on an IEP for Matthew.

When that day arrived, again we were hopeful because we felt we were moving in the right direction. The special-needs team had more experience with socially challenged children than the teachers at a school like Fresh Meadows; therefore, they would know how to redirect Matthew in order to help him focus. We were satisfied with the goals that were set and we signed off on them.

The hardest part of the meeting was when we discussed the option to have Matthew receive services in our home or at the school. Sonya and I were in agreement that he needed a little more space from us in order to start growing socially. The next decision was whether we wanted to drive him to and from school each day or let him ride a bus that would pick him up at our home at 7:00 a.m. and drop him back off at 11:30 a.m.

The thought of letting him ride the bus was troubling. Matthew was just nearing three years old, and he was still tiny. He could not tell us anything about his experiences or the people he was with. Sonya and I looked at each other and sat quietly. Sensing our hesitation, the program director informed us that the bus carried only a few children, and a driver's helper was on board to look after them. Matthew would be secured in a car seat for safety. She also reminded us he would only be gone for a few hours.

Having to make this decision brought to mind something a friend once told me about the first day her son took the bus to school. After putting her little boy on the bus, she at once got in her car and followed the bus to his school. When she told me this story, I thought she was going a bit too far, and I could not imagine why she ever even thought of doing such a thing. Now, I understood why. Yet, similar to when we enrolled Matthew in Fresh Meadows daycare, in spite of our fears, we chose what we thought was best for our little boy, and we let him take the bus. Matthew could not begin at the school until October when he was officially three years old, so Sonya and I had about three weeks to prepare ourselves. We were thankful for the time to talk it over more thoroughly and get comfortable with the idea of letting him go.

FINANCIAL SHIFTS AND CHANGES

IT WAS A weekday morning. I woke up at six thirty and tried not to think about how tired I was. Once I got going and stuck my head outside, the cool, light air passing by my door on its way across the street and into the nearby woods blew across my face and energized me. Sonya was squeezing out the last possible second of much-needed sleep, and Matthew was already up and playing in his bedroom upstairs. At the sound of me moving about in the kitchen, he decided to come down.

As Matthew descended the stairs, his radiant and playful face was preceded by the sound of his, "Hmsch, hmmmmm. Hmsch, hmmmmm. Hmsch, hmmmmm. Hmsch. hmmmmm.

Hmsch, hmmmmm...." The repetitive monotony of the single-toned noise, which he created by quickly inhaling through his nostrils and breathing out while sealing his lips, reminded me of a young child practicing a cymbal for hours following their first lesson—at first cute and tolerable, but in time, difficult to listen to.

We weren't sure why he did this, but, based on its frequency and consistency, it was clear he found it pleasing. Experts believed self-stimulating (or stimming, for short) behaviors such as humming, the flapping of hands, or nail biting provided autistic persons with the sensory input they craved while blocking the sensory experiences they disliked. In Matthew's case he hummed and mouthed things such as cloth, soft plastic items, or wooden blocks.

When he reached the bottom step and turned left to enter the living room, Matthew glanced in my direction and, without acknowledging my presence, picked up the toy horse at his feet to play. Then, in rhythm, Matthew continued stimming, "Hmsch, hmmmmm, Hmsch, hmmmmm." "Good morning Matthew," I said, waving my hands in the air to get his attention and to try to throw off the pattern of his comfort noise. In one rapid motion, he looked up and back down to his toy horse, "Hmsch, hmmmmm, Hmsch, hmmmmm, Hmsch, hmmmmm." I decided to take what I could get at that moment and not push for more. Over the next hour we ate breakfast, got dressed, and he and Sonya got into the car for their drive to a therapy appointment.

Once my wife's car was out of sight, I let out a deep sigh of relief that the first part of our morning drill was successfully completed on time. I gathered my thoughts to kick off the second half of the morning, which was thirty minutes of Bible study before a brisk three-mile walk around the neighborhood. My walks were partially for exercise but were mostly a time to pray. The benefits were immeasurable. Though there were times when I could not seem to clear my mind of the many things going on in our life, more often than not, talking to God about what was on my heart lifted the weight off my shoulders.

One of my biggest concerns was related to finances. I liked to believe I was too spiritually minded to worry about money—after all, did not the scripture say to not worry about what my family will eat or drink, or what we will wear (Matthew 6:33 NIV)? Was I so lacking in faith that I was not willing to believe God would meet our family's needs? And, why, after so many years of seeing Him bless me in unexplainable ways, was I still questioning? Let's just say I still had some growing to do.

We were spending a significant amount of money on uncovered health costs because our healthcare plan did not cover all of Matthew's therapy. Our household expenses exceeded our income, and we had already gone through our budget several times to cut every possible unnecessary cost. Our credit cards were running up well beyond what we could pay back at the end of each month. And, there was always something more Matthew needed. We were often forced to wrestle with choosing to take on more debt or not to give him what we believed would provide him the best chance to get well.

With no easy answers in sight, it was tempting to give in to worrying. For this reason, my time with God in the morning was not optional; rather, it was necessary more than ever. I read Philippians 4:6-8, which stated to "...not be anxious about anything, but in every situation, by prayer and petition, with thanksgiving, present your requests to God." It reminded me to pray to God for all of my family's needs, and it kept me from becoming distraught.

I regularly traveled from Atlanta to New Jersey for work, but, in recent months, there had not been much of a need for me to go. I did not mind because I preferred not to be away from my family; although, it was easy to feel disconnected from some of the larger, strategic planning that was happening at my company. It had recently been acquired by a bigger company, and there were organizational changes taking place. Many of the people whom I knew best either resigned or were laid off, and getting updates about what was happening in the office was not as easy as it had been in the past.

Along with my company's restructuring came a loss of job security for employees at many levels. It was common for senior managers, as well as regular staff, to be displaced due to global outsourcing efforts that were also taking place. It was a pins-and-needle climate, and I felt especially vulnerable working on my own from Georgia. I could not read the morale at the office or participate in water cooler conversations, which were often the source of company updates long before official memos were published.

In time, I heard rumors that my team might be on the radar for job cuts, but I had heard that type of talk for so long it was hard to know how to gauge it. Many times over the years, I had experienced the threat of losing my job amidst an environment of corporate and economic change. There was even a time when a company I was working for underwent so much restructuring that I kept my personal belongings packed at my desk, so, if terminated, I could leave at a moment's notice. Eventually, I adopted the philosophy that my best defense was to do an excellent job and not worry about the things I could not control.

The days of September were coming and going, and the rumors transformed into reality. After months of watching the size of my team shrink, I was notified that I was going to be laid off. My manager Jay was pretty torn apart when he called one morning to notify me; he felt I was doing a great job, but it was out of his hands. He was genuinely concerned about the consequences for my family. As I assured him things would be OK, I wondered how I would break the news to Sonya later that afternoon. The only bright side I could see was I would not be released for six weeks from the date I was notified. I would have time to try to find another job, even if it was not much time.

When I shared what was going on with Sonya, she was concerned, but she was faithful things would work out. Her industry, which was risk services, had more job openings than my business process outsourcing field, so we agreed she would search for jobs as well. We even considered this might prove to be a great opportunity for her to re-enter the workforce. We prayed together and prepared our minds to move forward with our plans. We were confident God would rescue us as always although we did not know how.

We began searching for work right away, and, as we had guessed, Sonya got leads quicker than I did. An interview with a well-known, large, risk services company forty-five minutes from our home, led to the hiring manager indicating to Sonya that she would certainly be receiving an offer. The salary was undetermined, but we were elated and relieved we would not have to go without income and medical insurance. Considering Matthew's needs, that would be extremely difficult.

Days later, in a follow up call, the hiring manager asked Sonya when she could start the position and assured her the offer letter would be mailed. We thanked God.

SEPTEMBER SURPRISE

THROUGH HEAVY RAIN and patches of fog, we returned home from an early morning doctor's appointment for Matthew. The northbound back road stretching from the main airport to our house covered only the second half of the hour-long trip back from midtown Atlanta. When we returned home in the opposite direction, the uninspiring weather left us feeling sluggish. If it had been Saturday, we would have been half-asleep under blankets on the couch and watching television.

In spite of the temptation to sit around and do nothing, Sonya seated herself at the dining room table to do some paperwork. I pulled up a chair nearby to search job sites using the same laptop I would soon have to turn in to my current employer. From the corner of my eye, I noticed that Sonya seemed restless. Eventually a look of discomfort settled on her face, and she put her head down on the table.

"Are you OK?" I asked.

"I'm not feeling so good," she answered, "I haven't been feeling well lately. I think I might need to see the doctor."

"Is it like cold symptoms?" I asked.

"Not really. I just feel kind of weak."

"You're probably just worn out from the late nights. It might be a good idea to try to get to sleep earlier tonight. Let's just shut things down earlier tonight, no matter what's going on. I'll get up when Matthew wakes up in the night."

Sonya slept through the night, but she still felt a little sick the next day. It was nothing that would stop her from going about her normal day; nonetheless, she still was not feeling great. We both figured she was just run down and in need of rest.

I thought about how often Sonya and I experienced cold or flu-like symptoms because our immune systems were working double time to keep up with the wear and tear of restless nights and stress. I felt exasperated as it occurred to me again that our life was unusually taxing, and occasional illnesses were an inescapable by-product of it. As my thinking began to spiral downward, I decided, instead of dwelling on the things that weren't going so well, I would be better off going to pick up over-the-counter medicine to relieve Sonya's discomfort.

My back landed heavily against the car seat. I felt groggy. Venturing back out in wet weather would not have been on my list of things to do, had it not been for the need at hand. I backed out of the garage slowly and turned on the radio, hoping to hear something to reroute my rainy-day mood. As I pulled out, I was surprised to see in spite of how bad the weather had been when we came home earlier, the sun had now come out.

There was not much to look at along the roads between our home and the supermarket, mostly trees and houses for the first few miles, then an occasional strip mall. Relaxing gradually, I cruised leisurely along the two-lane road. My mind drifted back to Sonya, and I wondered what I could buy, other than medicine, to lift her spirits—maybe something sweet to eat, flowers, or a good magazine.

As I drove along, trying to think of a magazine or flower Sonya might like, a staggering thought suddenly popped into my mind. It was as if unexpectedly a door was forcefully kicked open. I could hardly believe I had not considered it an hour earlier. Maybe it did not occur to me because of our focus on finding work. The thought was so profound that I turned the radio down and pulled the car to the side of the road. I examined it from every possible angle without coming up with a good reason to dismiss it—Sonya was pregnant.

We had stuck to the first part of our plan, which was to try for several months; however, by the beginning of July, there was no indication of conception, and we discussed resuming birth control, but we never did. We had good intentions but not a lot of conviction. By August, due to the hectic pace of our life, we no longer talked about pregnancy or another child. In a sense, the whole idea of getting pregnant slipped our minds.

The sensible approach to my premonition would have been not to jump to conclusions before talking with Sonya about taking a home pregnancy test or seeing her doctor. Nevertheless, in my heart of hearts, I was confident she was pregnant. I wondered how I could have missed the obvious, and I was sure if I had a hunch, Sonya definitely did too. I picked up the cell phone and called home,

"Hey," she answered.

"I'm calling because I just had the wildest idea about how you're feeling."

"What was it?"

"Do you think you could be pregnant?"

"It occurred to me, but I couldn't say for sure."

"Do you want me to pick up a test while I'm out?"

"You can."

"Ok, what if you're pregnant?"

"Well, I can take the home test, but we won't really know until I see the doctor."

"But what if you are? This would be strange timing; it's right when you're about to start working."

"God definitely has a sense of humor."

"That's for sure. Either way, I know it will all work out great. I'll see you when I get back in a few minutes."

Later on, a home pregnancy test indicated Sonya was pregnant and so did a doctor's visit. Soon after receiving confirmation, she began to have morning sickness, and she decided it would be neither right nor feasible for her to accept a position she could not manage from the outset. By that point she had not received her official offer letter, but she had been in contact with the hiring manager who communicated he was still obtaining the required approvals, but he was hoping to be able to send it soon. Sonya called him and let him know what was going on. He understood and told her he would love to hear from her once she was ready to reenter the workforce.

I reflected that, since Sonya was pregnant and could not work, and I had no job, then we would be pregnant and raising a special-needs child without an income. I thought there was no way this mix of miracle and test could not be from God. I saw it as a clear indication of His hand on our life, and, in a way that went against all my logical reasoning, I felt fortunate and could not wait to see what He would do next.

Chapter Four

DIAGNOSIS

IT HAD BEEN nine months since Sonya and I began observing Matthew with a heightened sense of concern. We were sure he had missed a number of significant toddler milestones. However, friends and family assured us this was common. "Your brother didn't start talking until he was three years old," my mother told me. My brother Gerald was two years younger than I was, and I could not remember him ever having any behavioral or speech issues. I was not completely convinced my mother's view applied to Matthew, but I held on to her optimistic words because she had successfully raised eight children. I desperately wanted to believe Matthew would similarly catch up and our worries would all come to nothing.

Since we had been living with my mother-in-law Theresa, she had plenty of opportunities to observe our son's behavior. Theresa felt a tremendous amount of grandmotherly pride, and she dearly loved her first and only grandchild. She would not utter one word about Matthew that was not positive or flattering. When she noticed that there was a hiccup in his progress, she reassuringly told us many boys start talking late. Though her words were comforting, they lacked conviction, and the fact that she felt the need to console us revealed she shared our concern that Matthew might be lagging compared to other children his age. Sonya and I also knew that while being able to take seriously any potential condition Matthew might have, Theresa would not allow some ailment to sidetrack her unconditional love for him.

Sonya and I had been on a harrowing search to find a doctor who could tell us whether Matthew had autism. Both of us had read as much as we could on the subject, and based on his lack of speech, short attention span, and limited eye contact we were becoming more and more convinced he had some form of an autism spectrum disorder. However, it was still just speculation; we needed an official diagnosis if we were going to obtain the right type of care for Matthew. We wanted to move past feeling vaguely bewildered and perplexed to finding out exactly what was holding Matthew back. However, for some reason it was not easy to secure a professional judgment.

Now, driving down the highway to the New Center for Autism Progress (also known as the New Center) in near silence, we were searching for answers. The early, afternoon sky was beautiful, with miles of blue between each cloud for as far as we could see. It was as if the fall had given the exiting summer permission to show off one last time. On any other day like this, Sonya and I would have felt inspired, but today was different. We had prayed together, talked through the questions we wanted to ask, and gathered every medical record we could find to help us describe what we saw happening with our three-year-old.

Sonya and I sensed the doctors, teachers, and therapists who had already seen Matthew, were holding something back from us. It seemed incongruous that one expert after another said they could help Matthew work through specific delays, but none of them could explain what was going on with him overall. We were sure that they had to know more about autism and developmental disorders than they were letting on. They worked with children all the time. Matthew could not have been the only three-year-old they had seen with these symptoms. We hoped to find a doctor at the New Center in Atlanta who could help us understand what was happening.

We thanked God for leading us to Dr. Childress and the New Center, which focused on children like Matthew. Dr. Childress, who appeared to be in her late forties, was a neurodevelopmental pediatrician and had been with the New Center for over a decade. Originally from the San Francisco Bay area, she obtained her education and training in Seattle. She was reserved, but I liked her demeanor. She had a confidence that reminded me of many people I knew back home in New Jersey.

Dr. Childress was one of the few doctors in the region who was capable of identifying autism, and qualified to diagnose it. Her career had been devoted to the research, treatment, and education of children with developmental issues stemming from a variety of causes. There was a months-long waiting list to see her, and Sonya and I took it as the helping hand of God that we were able to get Matthew an appointment within weeks from the time that we called the New Center. Matthew's autism evaluation was a two-day affair. On the first day, Sonya and I spent about two hours with Dr. Childress, providing medical background information on Matthew and our family and filling out forms.

On the following day, we brought Matthew along, and Dr. Childress attempted to interact with him using various age-appropriate activities and toys to gauge his responses. Matthew sought out the things he was interested in and sometimes, momentarily, appeared to engage Dr. Childress, but, for the most part, he barely acknowledged her. Matthew related to the world around him in a way only he understood.

Over the course of our hour with her, Dr. Childress took notes on Matthew's behavior. At the end of the appointment, she told us she would provide formal documentation that summed up her findings, but, based on the evaluation criteria, she was certain Matthew did have autism. She said he appeared to be neither high functioning nor severe, but was somewhere in the middle of the spectrum. I felt numb inside. I wondered what this really meant for the future as I unsuccessfully tried to understand, even in part, what God might be doing.

As we were leaving the evaluation room, I paused in the doorway. Sonya was already in the hall. I knew I was fishing for reassurance, but I turned back to Dr. Childress and asked her if, based on what she had seen with other children, she thought Matthew could overcome this. Now that I was no longer feeling dazed, I hoped to hear something to take away the sting of the words we had just heard—reassurance she had seen plenty of children like Matthew, and, with the proper treatment, he would be fine. Her response was sympathetic, but honest. "We really don't know," she said. I guess I had known the answer to my question before I asked it.

In the following days, it was hard to make sense of what was happening. We knew for sure that Matthew had autism, but I did not know whether to feel relieved or more concerned. In terms of finding help, it was a step in the right direction, but the diagnosis also closed the door on any sliver of hope we had that this was all just a bad dream, and one day we would wake up to find Matthew on track and speaking to us like any other toddler.

Sonya and I became more fixated on searching for information to help Matthew than on sorting out our feelings about what was taking place. It felt like a hurricane-strength wind was blowing through our home, leaving our lives completely upended. Autism instantly consumed our thinking and our conversations day and night, twenty-four hours a day, seven days a week. We were unable to focus on anything else. Matthew having autism was a crisis.

I did not understand the ins and outs of the complex disorder, but it seemed as though it had the potential to alter the blueprint Sonya and I had for our family's future. My wife and I loved God and had spent the better part of our adult lives focused on serving Him. I knew God said "in all things He works for the good of those who love him, and who have been called according to his purpose" (Romans 8:23), yet as I considered what was happening I wondered what good could come from Matthew having a life-changing illness. Nevertheless, I recalled all I had seen God do for me and for Sonya over the years: how he changed our lives and gave us a purpose; how He brought us together to be married; and how He had always taken care of us, especially through Sonya's difficult pregnancy with Matthew.

As quickly as I settled my mind through these truths, another flurry of questions swept through me. Matthew was not talking like other children his age. Would he ever? He ran around with little concern about where Sonya or I were. Would this go on forever? Would Matthew and I be able to exchange thoughts someday? My uneasiness became so overwhelming I had to sit and quietly remind myself of what I knew to be true and what I really believed. "God is here," I softly but firmly told myself. "He sees our situation. He knows and understands what we are going through. He loves and cares for Sonya, Matthew and me. He helps us. He works in His time. His plans and perspective are greater than mine."

I understood no more about Matthew's future or which way our life was headed, but I was convinced that even in this darkest of clouds, God was loving, and, beyond the shadow of a doubt, He could bring good from what we were going through. From what I had known and experienced throughout my sixteen years of walking with God, with Him, change, whether good or bad, is not the end, rather it is a new beginning. Knowing this did not make our situation any less sad, and I did not believe God wanted Sonya and me to gloss over our emotions, but if our family was going to make it through this and live out the purpose He had for us, I knew we had to keep our eyes on Him.

Chapter Five

NOT BY SIGHT

Consider it pure joy, my brothers and sisters, whenever you face trials of many kinds, because you know that the testing of your faith produces perseverance.

- James 1:2
(NIV)

THE SUN HAD yet to come up and the moon was still glowing on the first October morning Matthew was to be picked up by bus to attend the early intervention program. I turned on our driveway floodlights, and he, Sonya, and I waited patiently in the dining room. We periodically looked through the blinds to see if the bus was approaching. Matthew's backpack was almost as big as his body, and he was ready to go the moment the bus arrived. Within minutes, the massive, yellow and black transport bellowed as it turned the corner from the main road and illuminated our property with its large headlights. It came to a halt, and, the door opened. Attempting to recover from the glare, I squinted and placed my hand above my brow to catch a glimpse of the driver's face before putting Matthew on the bus.

The bus driver's name was Rachel. In time, we got to know her as a kind and gentle-spirited person, which we found comforting. I was sure that if the bus door had opened and I did not like the look of the driver, I would have pulled my son back and taken him to school myself. I lifted Matthew's body up to each step because, though he could come down the stairs in our home, he did not yet know how to walk up them; and, even if he was able to, the bus steps were too high for his undersized legs. Momentarily, I realized that this was a whole new chapter of life for us, and it was just days after Matthew had turned three. This was not easy.

After watching the red and orange rear lights of the bus vanish around the same corner as it had appeared and hearing the sound of its engine diminishing, Sonya and I went in the house, prayed, and cried. Weeks later, after we had become better acquainted with Rachel, she told us that she identified with how we must have felt. She told us she could not believe how small Matthew was the first time she picked him up, and she wondered if she could have let a child of her own, at that age, ride a bus. I appreciated Rachel's empathy, yet felt our decision to send Matthew to the program was the right one. I also regularly drove to the school to peek in on Matthew through the window of his classroom door.

AMONG FAMILIAR COMPANY

WHEN THE HOLIDAY season came around, our family pulled up to the front of River Pond Middle School surprised to see so many cars in the well-lighted parking lot. It appeared to be nearly full. I had been wrong in assuming that because the special education department's Christmas party took place on a weeknight, a large number of parents would pass on it. The school-sponsored event was intended to give the families of their special education students a chance to mix and mingle in a festive environment amidst seasonal activities, refreshments and a classic looking Santa with whom the children could take photographs.

Initially, I felt some apprehension about going to the gathering. Matthew only weighed twenty pounds and stood less than three feet tall, but he was impulsive and hard to manage. His eyes were restless; Matthew relentlessly followed his eyes, suddenly and frequently changing his direction with little awareness of what he was leaving behind or what lay ahead in his path. After about an hour or so of following Matthew around, step for step, to prevent him from running out of an exit door or pulling a bowl full of red fruit punch off of a table, Sonya and I were ready to go.

We split the duty of tracking Matthew however and ended up staying for a little while longer - about an hour and a half. Keeping up with him made it difficult to hold conversations, but we managed to have a good time in spite of it and found the party uplifting. We spoke with some parents, but mostly we took in the opportunity to observe other families who resembled ours. Until that night's event, we had not seen many, if any at all. Though most appeared to be doing far less chasing of their children around the room than we were, we soaked in the feeling of belonging that came from seeing other people who were experiencing the same things with their children as we were. Before leaving, we had Matthew take his first photo with Santa. It helped us to be there.

AN EXCEPTIONAL CHRISTMAS

DECEMBER'S ATMOSPHERE ALMOST always provided an opportunity not to focus on the many adversities competing for our attention. My severance had just run out, and I did not have any promising job prospects. For the moment, our income was officially unemployment income insurance, which would run out in less than a month. The only thing I was sure of was that God still saw us and was going to do something about our situation.

It was hard to determine exactly what would create an enchanted Christmas for Matthew that year. Would he enjoy a train ride through the woods as we had done in the past, or should we do a drive-through light show because of his sensory challenges? Would he love a particular electronic learning toy as a gift, or would we find out later he just wanted the colorful box it was packaged in. Things such as how to engage him and deciding whether to travel and manage him at someone else's house or just stay home began to take more thought.

Before we had a child, my wife and I assumed that once we did, the days and weeks leading up to Christmas would be marked by holding off a badgering child filled with wonder, but that was not a part of our current reality. Matthew would gladly play with whatever toys we gave him, but until the moment they were in his hands, he had no idea that they were coming. Sonya and I did not need to sneak toys into the house or stay up late to wrap them. There was no need to hide them for weeks ahead— the way my parents did when I was a kid. For us, Christmas was becoming far less about what gifts we gave or received, or which family members we visited, and more about establishing a holiday practice that Matthew could relate to and participate in.

Our family's special needs even impacted the way we talked to others about Christmas. My friend, Leigh, had more enthusiasm about the holidays than just about anyone I had ever known. I met her when we worked on a project together months before Sonya and I got married. She was a family-oriented woman who had two elementary-age sons. Unlike me, she was someone who loved the shopping, decorating, card writing, cooking, parties, and every other characteristic of the second half of December. I got the impression that she secretly dreamt about it all year long.

"So are you ready for Christmas yet?" Leigh inquired. Through the phone, I could feel her eyes light up and sense her anticipation of sitting with her family as they tore off the wrapping paper from their gifts. There was no doubt in my mind that she got a thrill just from thinking about Christmas morning. On one hand, her child-like posture was refreshing and possibly contagious. On the other hand, I could not identify with her enthusiasm at all.

"Not quite," I replied hesitantly, "I've been a last-minute shopper my whole life. I guess I like it that way."

"But you know what you're getting everybody, right?" Leigh was trying to believe in me, but I doubted that I would not disappoint her.

"Not yet," I answered trying to figure how many days were left until Christmas Day. I did not want to reveal too much of my thinking— partly out of concern about raining on Leigh's holiday parade and partly out of concern about being a killjoy during our conversation. "I don't usually get super fired up about Christmas. It's not that I don't like it. ...I mean I do, but it's not like I long for it either. I usually get excited on Christmas Eve."

Leigh was eager to awaken the hidden, holiday spirit in me. "But oh my goodness, what about Matthew? I bet he must be going nuts waiting for Christmas, huh? My boys were so excited when they were his age. They couldn't wait."

The instantaneous sadness aroused in me by her completely normal comment was independent of rational thinking. Leigh had met Matthew when he was a baby, and I had since shared with her that he had autism. Like me, prior to Matthew's diagnosis, she did not understand what autism was. I attempted to compose myself in order to avoid sounding as if something was wrong. It was difficult, because my mind was now fixed on trying to envision what it would be like if Matthew comprehended the concept of Christmas.

"He doesn't really understand it yet," I said, fearing a second comment from Leigh that might make me reluctant to continue our conversation.

"Oh, that's OK," she replied, oblivious to the deliberation that had just taken place on the other end of the phone, "my boys did not get it either when they were really small. Believe me, he'll get it," she chuckled. "Enjoy it before he gets older and starts asking for everything." I wondered to myself whether or not Matthew would ever get it, and I thought about how much I would love it if he asked me for everything.

FINDING OUR COMMUNITY HOME

IT WAS WITHIN a couple of months of starting in the county school program, that Matthew was also accepted into the early intervention program at the New Center for Autism Progress. For a number of weeks, he had participated in both programs at half-day intervals, but soon after, he was admitted to the New Center on a full-time basis. From then on, we maintained an IEP with the local school system, just in case we needed to return to using their services at some point in the future, but we pulled him out of his attendance in River Pond Middle School's early intervention program.

Our decision to move Matthew to the New Center full time was not only because Dr. Childress provided us with the diagnosis of autism, but also because, at that time, the New Center was more innovative in their knowledge, treatment, and their continuous learning efforts about autism, than was the school system. Whereas our public school system was reluctant to engage us in a conversation about the possibility of Matthew having autism, the New Center specialized in addressing it.

For the next three years of our life, the New Center would be paramount to Matthew's behavioral treatment, and become the center of the autism community to which our family would belong.

Matthew was now more of a budding preschooler than a baby, and his progress since the previous year's Christmas was noticeable, though not monumental. I thought about the meaning of his name, "Small Gift of God," and how it fit perfectly with the theme of the season. At the time, I struggled with the idea of autism as a gift, but I was sure, that, in some way that only God knew, Matthew would someday live up to his name.

LIFTED UP

BEFORE WE KNEW it, it was almost February, and we were heading into our seventh month without work. I had seen God work out situations many times over the years, but I had no insight as to when and how he would resolve this one. I could only stick to what I knew to be true and diligently do the things that I believed were most effective. I wished that I was the person who prayed and never wavered in their thinking, but I could not make that claim. I believed, but some days my faith was steadier than other days. Most days, I would be crystal clear about the fact that God was intimately concerned about our situation, but there were other times when I battled discouragement —wondering what I needed to do next, and what if...?

Sundays were the one day of the week that I rarely struggled to believe that everything would be fine. I attended church in the morning and was almost always encouraged by the message that was preached or the conversations I had with other Christians after the service. On one particular Sunday that month, the teaching was on faith — specifically asking God for what we need, and then believing the request is granted, regardless of what things seem like. The moral of the lesson was, if we believe that we have what we asked for, then our actions should reflect that belief.

As a result, I decided to be faithful and to ask God to let me know where I would be working by the end of that week. I decided to trust enough to act simply as if I already had a job. I went home and told Sonya our financial drought was over, and I would be working by the end of the week. I also communicated my expectations by email to Janice, a former colleague and friend. On Wednesday, January 10, 2007, at 10:15 AM, I sent Janice a message:

I wrote: Hi Janice, I heard back from [A company I interviewed with] again today and [Another company] at the end of last week. I will be working by Friday this week, and will continue to look at bigger positions from there.

Janice replied: You will be working by Friday this week?, Wow! That is excellent news. What will you are doing?

I replied: "I don't know yet. I believe it by faith. I will update you when it happens."

Janice wrote back: Okay, great. Yes, please let me know. That's great that you are getting callbacks also. Keep me posted.

I read her response and thought that it seemed like she had to make an effort to not to feel sorry for me, or try to help me stay realistic about how to search for jobs. I could hear her thinking, "Oh no, he has gotten so desperate that he is starting to make up jobs."

I replied: I know you're thinking, "He's crazy," but let's see. Talk to you soon.

Throughout the week, I continued to look through job postings and to call anybody with whom I could network or who might know of something. I did not think I was supposed to just sit home and wait for a position to come through the door. However, each day brought nothing. I even interviewed for two jobs that week and both fell through.

On Friday morning, in spite of the lack of good news, I woke up thinking, "Today is the day that I am going to find work because this is what I have asked God for." This mindset and confidence was not usual for me. Normally, I would put on an air about me as if I really believed and tried to ignore the little voice in my head questioning whether or not it would really happen. On that particular Friday, I was relaxed, confident, and excited. I prayed and asked God to show me where the job was that he already had lined up for me, and then I kept my eyes and ears open, looking for any type of a lead, no matter how big or small.

When the phone rang later that morning, I ran to grab it. It was my friend, Felicia, whom I spoke with from time to time. We had met at my former company where she was still employed. Felicia had called just to say hello and to catch up. At one point in our conversation, she asked me how my job search was coming along. I told her things were slow, but I was expecting something big to happen very soon. In passing, she said that she had heard that the project I was working on, which was previously canceled, was back on. She suggested I contact my former manager.

I took Felicia's remark as if it came from God, and I knew I had to act on it. Immediately, I called my former manager. He was the same person who had called me in September to let me know that my position had been eliminated. His phone rang a few times and then went straight to voice mail, so I left a message, "Hi Jay, this is Paul Powell. I heard there might be a chance the offshore project is back on, and people might be needed. I was calling to see if you had any information about it, and to get your opinion on whether or not you think I should call the senior manager about it."

Within a couple of hours my phone rang and it was Jay. He was lighthearted and friendly,

"Hi Paul, how are you?"

"I'm good."

"I got your message."

"Yes, I spoke to someone who mentioned that the Overstreet project might be getting some attention again. Since I still haven't found anything, I wanted to get your advice on whether or not you think I should call Mark."

"It's funny that you happened to call today," he replied, " I just came out of a meeting with Mark's boss, and he told me that he was committed to getting the Overstreet project going again and asked what I needed in order to do that. I told him that I needed you back. He completely understood and said he is fully behind it. I think you should call Mark."

I hung up with Jay and called Mark. I left a brief message on his voice mail, and then sent him an email message:

Hi, Mark, I tried to reach you by phone, but you were in a meeting. As I have continued to network, interview, and seek positions, I have periodically checked the JCC career Web site for rehire opportunities. I have reviewed opportunities within [the office] but have been unable to find a fit for my skill set. I am also investigating retraining options to make my skill set a better fit for the current market. That being said, I am not sure where your project strategy stands, but I thought it might be worth asking you if there is any opportunity for me to rejoin JCC, supporting your offshore efforts in any capacity. Can you please let me know when I might be able to reach you by phone to discuss it further? Thanks.

Mark got back to me and, within a few days, interviewed me. I was rehired at over ten thousand dollars more per year than my salary had been when I was laid off six months earlier. My benefits were also treated as if they were never interrupted, so I lost none of the vacation time I had built up when I was laid off. Sonya and I were relieved and happy. Some people might call the whole thing coincidence, but I knew that God saw our situation, and He did something about it.

On Thursday, February 1, 2007, at 5:07:48 PM, I received an email message from Janice, inquiring about my job search:

Janice wrote: Any update? I thought about you and wanted to get an update to see how it is going?

I replied: Well, you know I prayed to have a job by that Friday.... I am back at JCC... I found out on that exact day.... the salary increase that came with it is the answer to something that I had been praying for months. God is awesome.

I sat back, reflected for a moment, and thought about how difficult the past six months had been and how the rigors of our life and Matthew's needs made it even tougher. I felt the weight of the sadness and sense of loss that existed inside my wife, and I pictured Matthew, who, though happy, was on a course of adversity. There had been many times over the last half year when, deep down inside, I felt the temptation to question what God was doing with our family. I now felt a great sense of gratitude for what He had done for us, and my trust in Him was strengthened.

Chapter Six

MOURNING IN MARRIAGE

The Lord is close to the brokenhearted and saves those who are crushed in spirit.

- Psalm 34:18
(NIV)

SONYA AND I sat on the couch with the space of a person between us. We had reached a point of silence, each feeling unheard by the other. "I just think we need to accept the fact that our life is not about our plans anymore—at least not for now," I said.

Sonya's tone rivaled mine, "We already gave up everything we could. We have to have a life, or we will burn out. I feel like I'm already close to my limit."

"Matthew didn't ask to have autism, and he didn't ask to be born," was my quick rebuttal.

"I don't think that's the point. We're talking about keeping a balance between taking care of him and taking care of us. We have to accept the fact that we can only do so much. We have to take care of our own health and everything else."

"I have accepted it, but I still think we can do more than what we're doing. We owe that to Matthew."

"You're saying two things at once," she said. "We're not getting anywhere. Let's just drop it for now."

I was bothered because I felt she cut off the conversation, but inside I knew there was no resolution to be had at the moment. We were both upset and not in a mindset to compromise. Our marriage was strong, and we worked well together, but the tension and complexities accompanying autism sometimes caught up with us. Also, Sonya was pregnant at the time, and, though the pregnancy was going well, it would have been a mistake for me to add any more burdens to the many concerns already on her mind.

It had taken more than a year to get an official, documented diagnosis; once we did, it seemed to have a domino effect of trials on other areas of our lives and on us. Matthew was settled in at the New Center, but his progress would not be as simple as sending him off every morning and waiting for him to come home one afternoon speaking in sentences. I somehow expected things would get easier after receiving clarification on Matthew's condition. I envisioned the diagnosis as step one of a well-designed program we could put in place to get Matthew where he needed to be. I seriously underestimated the undercurrent of strains that came with the pursuit of his healing—and ours.

GETTING IN TOUCH

THAT WEEK, SUNDAY service was held in a large hotel. After worship ended, fellowship began. Everyone always seemed inspired after listening to Sunday's message, and this Sunday was no different. On my way out, at the top of the escalator, I ran into Ross. He was a physician and an old friend of Sonya's. Originally from the Caribbean, Ross had lived in the United States for many years. He was a well-dressed, tall, African-American man with glasses and a short, graying beard. He and Sonya met when they led a campus ministry together during college. He was as devoted a Christian as I had ever met.

"Hey Ross, how are you?" I was feeling pretty inspired myself.

"Hey Bro'. How ya doing?" Ross smiled genuinely.

"'I'm good."

"Where's Sonya?"

I felt pressure to answer in the right way. Church attendance had once been a huge measure of someone's spirituality in our congregations, and, even though things had changed, old habits die hard. It used to be someone needed a very good reason to miss a service.

"She's home resting," I said (which was the absolute truth).

"How is your son doing?" Ross knew Matthew had autism.

"He's doing well, but it's hard sometimes. There is a lot that goes into getting him help. It's a lot of time and money. It can be taxing."

"I'm sure." He replied, lowering his brow empathetically. He continued, "Grieving over loss is a process that takes time."

His words caught me off guard. *"Loss? What loss?"* I thought to myself. *"My son is not dead."* The look on my face shifted from reflective to puzzled, and I tried to link what we were going through at home to the words that Ross had just spoken. Sensing my confusion, he put his hands up as if to say "Don't get me wrong," and quickly attempted to reassure me. "What I meant is not that you literally lost your son, you still have him with you; rather, it is the loss of the son whom you thought you were going to have. In the same way some people experience the loss of a loved one who passes away, others with family members who have an illness can go through a time of grieving." I sensed he spoke from a sincere, professional, and personal perspective; even though I could not understand what he was saying in relation to my family at that moment, I took his words to heart.

After we talked for another minute or so, I hurried down the escalator past many faces I knew and out to my car on the parking deck. I could not remember much of the sermon because my mind was now on Ross's comment. I wondered if

I were grieving, but unaware of it. Was I deeply sad, but out of touch? I tried to consider all of the things I wanted to do with Matthew but were now not possible, to see if they made me feel like a grief-stricken person. I felt nothing. I tried to think of anything I was sad about that we could not do together, "Baseball? No. Bike riding? Maybe. Painting and drawing? No, not really." Something in Ross's words rang true for me, but I did not know what it was. Was I angry? Could I have been emotionally shutdown? I honestly did not know.

REACHING THE END OF THE LINE

I HAD FULLY made up *my* mind we were going to do whatever was necessary to get Matthew well. I had read about families with an autistic child, in which the husband checks out emotionally, or worse—leaves his family because he can't handle the situation. I believed we owed it to our son, no matter how much personal anguish it caused us, not to give up or let up. I believed we were in a battle to save Matthew, and, with all of the work needing to be done, there was no room for anyone to be hurt, except Matthew—certainly not me, and certainly not Sonya. This attempt at noble heroics prevented me from connecting with my wife and being in touch with her during a time that almost broke her spirit.

From a practical and task-oriented standpoint, I was doing everything I could to take as much pressure off of Sonya as possible. But that was not what she really needed. Sonya was being squeezed on all sides. Early intervention for Matthew had previously taken a physical toll on her because his educational programs were split between two different schools forty miles apart; each requiring him to be there three hours a day. We used to put him on the bus for River Pond in the morning, and, three hours later, Sonya picked him up and drove him to the

New Center on the north side of Atlanta. Once there, she used the next three hours to run errands, shop, or grab something to eat before picking him up and driving forty miles back home. When we moved him to the New Center full-time, Sonya was now driving 160 miles a day, five days a week. Add to this the therapy and physician appointments, along with the other normal demands of being a wife and mother, and it was too much.

One evening, after we had finally gotten Matthew to sleep, we turned on the television and tried to relax. Insomnia was a part of autism, and we knew by now it was just a matter of time before Matthew woke up again. We had no illusions we would sleep through the night. A full night's sleep was no longer a part of our life. It probably would have been more prudent to get in bed early ourselves to get a head start, but it was too irresistible to pass up any opportunity to relax in a peaceful environment: one absent of the nonstop humming sounds Matthew made to comfort himself.

One of my favorite ways to wind down was watching football. I looked forward to the games so I could just sit on the couch, snack on something sweet or salty, and get lost in the competition. During the most difficult times of the day, the thought of watching a game in the evening brought me joy, not only because of the game itself, but also because I equated watching it to a stress-free experience. Every day contained more pressure than I cared for, and watching football was as carefree an activity as I could think of. It was entertaining, and, unlike a drama, suspense movie, or even a sitcom, it did not require me to think or talk. Sonya, on the other hand, usually relaxed at the end of the evening by connecting with a friend or family member on the phone. Tonight, however, she wanted to talk with me.

The television in our bedroom was on as she entered through the doorway and walked to the side of the bed opposite of where

I was sitting. Her body language—slow movement, slumped shoulders, and head down—conveyed she felt troubled. The television, situated on top of a dresser, was surrounded by decoratively framed photos of us on our honeymoon. I was parked on top of our comforter with pillows under my lower back and the television remote in hand. My back sighed with relief, no longer balancing the weight of my body, and I could feel my chest muscles letting go of the day's tension as worries began to slip away and my interest in the game grew.

I knew my wife, and, aside from feeling something was not right in recent weeks—if not months—I had clearly seen the decline in her energy level and demeanor as she fought to keep a make-the-best-of-it attitude. Even before her first words were spoken, I felt uneasy, anticipating what was coming. I was almost certain I would feel overwhelmed by whatever she was about to share. I could also tell it was hard for her to talk about whatever was on her mind.

"I don't feel good," she said, her eyes filling with tears. She was probably hoping I would pick up on her signals and spare her from having to spell out for me that I needed to disengage from the television and focus on her. I felt my chest start to tighten again.

"What's happening?" I asked.

"I don't know. I just think it's all too much. I'm really sad."

At these words, I instantaneously went from completely relaxed to overwhelmed and anxious, but I remained available to talk.

Taking my hand, she continued to speak, "I need an outlet. I can't do the driving schedule every day. It's too much. It takes up my whole day, and I think I need to do something constructive that lets me interact with people and be productive."

"What do you think is the answer?" I was not aware of the lack of compassion my response was transmitting.

"I don't know. I just need a break!"

"Maybe I can work out a way to drive him sometimes," I said. Even though I had known the stress was too much for her, I pulled away from fully embracing what she was saying because I reasoned if she did not drive Matthew, then he could not get the help he needed; therefore he could not get well. I worked during the day, and the distance and cost of the daily trips did not make a transportation service realistic. It was hard for me to get past feeling if I supported my wife, I would be failing my son.

Somewhere deep down inside of me, I wanted to reassure Sonya of my love for her and insist she forget about carting Matthew all over Atlanta, but I did not. Instead, I tried to put a patch on the situation, hoping she would be able to hold on until our life eased up. My thinking was unrealistic. Sonya was overwhelmed, not only by the demands of her day that left little or no time to work through this experience, but also because she was suffering from the repercussions of everything that had happened since she had gotten pregnant. I was severely underestimating how long it would be before our life got easier. Autism treatment was not a sprint, rather it was a marathon.

"I think it would help to see somebody."

Sonya's words hit my ears, and I realized my perception of what was happening to her and what it would take to make things better was still way off. Was I that shallow and distant?

"It might be good for you to talk to somebody if you think it would help," I said, at the same time wondering what would be required of me.

"I'm talking about a professional therapist," she added, to make sure that I was getting her point.

I felt anxious as I pictured her in a room with a stranger saying things about me I did not want shared.

"I know. I think you're right. I don't know exactly what they do, but I can't imagine it would do anything but help. Maybe we could at least find out what we can do to make things better."

Sonya was crying harder now, and I was feeling like a fish out of water.

"I think it might help me just to be able to talk to someone," she said.

I wondered why I could not offer her what she needed. I wished I could be the hero. I wanted to fix everything and make our life perfect. Isn't that what men are supposed to do for their families? Why was mine falling apart?

"I never felt this way before," she commented.

"When is the last time you remember feeling better?"

Sonya paused, thought for a moment, and answered, "Probably before Matthew was born. I just think it's been so much to work through and make sense of. So much of my life has changed so fast. I feel like I don't know if I am coming or going."

As Sonya continued to talk, I saw her pain, and I let down my defenses. A light was coming on for me. I was no longer thinking about whether or not I was missing a football game or if we could run the game plan I had in mind for Matthew. My wife was carrying a load that was much too heavy for her, and we were going to be in deep trouble if something did not change quickly.

GETTING HELP TO GO ON

SONYA SCHEDULED AN appointment with a local counselor. We were both nervous and not exactly sure what to expect. I was concerned the doctor would not understand what she was really dealing with. I wondered what would happen if she had a bad experience. Would that make matters worse? "Maybe I should go with her?" I thought. After discussing it, we decided she would go alone and ask the therapist whether or not it was appropriate for me to come next time and if that would be beneficial or detrimental to Sonya's treatment.

I walked Sonya out to the garage with Matthew right behind me and watched as she got into our car and backed out of the driveway. I hoped her session would go quickly and she would return home soon with good news about how promising it was. The sky was gray, and it was raining heavily outside, so it took extra effort not to feel a little sad and to believe sincerely the session would go well. As she pulled out of the driveway and turned the corner, I felt thankful I had Matthew there to keep me company.

The garage door rumbled down and I turned to look at Matthew. He had his hands over his ears and was backing through the laundry room into the living room. Lately, he was beginning to speak more, but most of it was echolalia—repeating the last word spoken by someone else.

"Mommy is going to be back soon." I said to him, imagining he would answer me in a complete sentence.

"Back soon," he responded.

"She went to the doctor," I went on, not knowing how much he understood.

"Doctor"

"Yes, the doctor."

"Doctor," he interjected with a slight smile looking off to the light fixture on the chandelier.

"So what should we do while she is gone?" I asked.

"Gone," he repeated, turning toward the television.

"Let's eat."

"Eat."

"Ok," I said, purposely prompting him to close out the conversation.

"Ok."

TURNING POINT

OUR PRAYERS WERE answered. When Sonya returned a couple of hours later, although she was not ecstatic, she was hopeful. It seemed Sonya really would benefit from the opportunity to talk to someone about what she had been through and the resulting grief she was experiencing. To my surprise and discomfort, the therapist was a man. His name was Les. To my delight, he was a Christian who shared similar values as ours and counseled from a spiritual viewpoint. In this first session, he listened to Sonya's history including her experience working in the World Trade Center during the terrorist attack on 9/11, her pregnancy, and all that happened with Matthew since his birth. He reassured her by simply saying, "With all that has taken place, how could you not be suffering as a result?"

As Sonya told me about her session, I could see the weight on her heart had lessened after Les confirmed her feelings were legitimate. She was not crazy, and she was not supposed to be strong enough to just get over it and carry on with life as usual—no less a life that involved caring for a special-needs child. Subsequent to Sonya sharing with Les that she had not been able to handle even routine household tasks because she felt so overwhelmed, he encouraged her from a spiritual standpoint by reminding her God did not want her to live her life on a shelf, and He still had big plans for her in the future. I think I got as much help from the session as Sonya.

11:00 PM. that same night was the time the college football game I was watching ended. Sonya and I had just climbed into bed. The day had been as good and as free of issues as was possible in our household. I did not feel particularly pensive about anything, but I was looking forward to calling it a day. Sonya put down the magazines she had been reading. As I lifted the blanket to get in the bed, I said something in passing, which I had been uttering a lot lately without giving much thought to it, "I'm glad this day is over. The end of the day is better than the beginning."

"What do you mean by that?" Sonya asked.

I was surprised and unprepared to stop and think about my words, so I answered instinctively.

"Because I feel like I made it through today, and tomorrow has new possibilities."

"So do you enjoy your days?"

"I don't know. I think so. Why do you ask?"

There was no pause for breath between my question and Sonya's answer, "Because you seem kind of frustrated lately. So I was wondering how you were feeling."

I did not like where the conversation was going because I would have to think about how I felt. "Hmmm," I stopped to consider what she was saying, "No, I think I'm OK. Everything is not where I want it to be, but I can't complain."

"Ok," she said, "good night."

"Sleep well," I said as I turned off the light, feeling unsettled because I knew there was some truth to what Sonya was saying.

At 2:00 AM, I woke up from a dream with my arms wrapped around my wife, clinging to her and sobbing uncontrollably. She leaned her head on me, and I cried and cried and cried without speaking. The dam had broken, and, in the absence of words, we both knew why. Processing what it meant for Matthew to have autism was almost unbearable, and circumventing dealing with it on an emotional level was impossible. Like a tide of rushing water crashing against the same place again and again, it could only be held back for so long.

Sonya was relieved to see there was still a feeling person inside me. "It's OK," she whispered in my ear. Just remember you don't have to do it alone." Her words were, in a sense, prophetic to what I believe God wanted me to understand.

It was hard for me to accept the realization that, even though we did our best to live a good Christian life, our family was not exempt from depression, illness, or heartaches. I had to face the fact that what we were dealing with could not be overcome by "white-knuckling" it. Some things were bigger than me, and, no matter how much I wanted life to be perfect for our family, there would be days when we would feel sad and cry; and I could do little to change it. And, though I wanted Matthew to be rid of autism, the treatments we were utilizing took time and carried no promises of results—no matter how hard I pushed for them.

I could not prevent days in which it felt like the vast, blue sky God created was falling before my eyes. All I could do was pray and remember Jesus' words "Blessed are those who mourn, for they will be comforted." (Matthew 5:4 NIV), and know by faith, I really was. I had experienced it before during some of the toughest times in my life and was now experiencing it again. At a time when the weight of life was clearly too hard for me to manage alone, God carried and comforted our family, far beyond what I could ever fully understand.

Chapter Seven

SEARCHING FOR A CURE

IN THE FIRST week in May, our daughter, Jaida, was born healthy and even more beautiful than we had imagined. My euphoria began the moment she came into the world and did not go away. Her birth was a magnificent event that lifted our spirits and reinvigorated our family. It ushered in a peaceful period in which everything in our home seemed a little easier. Sonya and I celebrated with our relatives and took advantage of the opportunity to slow down and reconnect with friends.

On the day Jaida was born, our family spent hours together at the hospital admiring her. In the evening, as the sun began to set, I set out to drive home with Matthew so Sonya and Jaida could rest. Within thirty minutes, we were home and Matthew was sound asleep in bed. I walked from room to room turning off all the lights. I then went to my bedroom, and climbed into bed, feeling a sense of pride about being the father of two children. I tried to envision what life was going to be like as a family of four. As my head sank down into the pillow, I forgot that Matthew had developmental delays, and, not so long ago, I had been out of work. Those things seemed far away now, and, for a brief moment, I wondered if I was already asleep and dreaming.

ACTION

SOME PARENTS AND special-needs practitioners talked of viewing persons with autism as simply having a different approach to life than other people and not being disabled at all. I did not buy that. I would love to sit and talk with my son about all that was on his mind, but I could not, because he could not. I believed autism was clearly a disability, and, though I saw the good in Matthew, I could never imagine thinking of his disability as a new "normal."

There was never a day I did not want the disconnected look in Matthew's eyes to go away—that dazed stare indicating his attention was completely focused on whatever was going through his own mind, unaware of the world around him. I cherished the moments when he was able to look me in the eyes and reply to a question. I prayed constantly for Matthew to be rid of autism. They were prayers beyond number, delivered unrelentingly from as far back as I could remember. I wanted my son back, and I had asked God for a miracle. I was certain He knew my heart on this matter. I was so sure of this that at times, I seriously wondered where He was. What could God be thinking, and why did He not swiftly reach down to relieve Matthew's suffering and ours? I knew it was ridiculous for me to have such thoughts with all that I had seen God do in recent months by providing for us, and giving us Jaida, but dealing with the temptation to doubt was no one-round fight.

As our understanding of autism grew, so did our desire to see Matthew recover from it. It became an unquenchable longing for me, and it took our family down countless paths in search of a cure—each with its own unique trials and lessons. Autism awareness and research was growing rapidly on an international scale, and it seemed as if every other day new treatments were touted as effective remedies to help children on the spectrum improve their development. Though we were eager for help, we were just as concerned about being set up for a letdown or being taken advantage of. We knew we were vulnerable to scams that appealed to our emotions, and we were especially on our guard against any organization or practitioner claiming they could completely heal autism, often at a price well beyond what we could afford. We tried to pursue only those courses of action offering extensive data and case studies, and, even then, we knew there might be limitations on what we could do.

I spent many late nights with my head buried in books about autism or on the web hunting for clues to what was truly helping children improve, if *not* fully recover. The number of medical journals, independent articles, blogs, and chats available to comb through was overwhelming. Many of the sites raised as many questions as answers, but they also offered something unexpected and tremendously helpful—personal stories from parents describing symptoms we had previously only encountered with Matthew, such as body temperature changes, insomnia, and aversions to or cravings for certain textures.

I found an instant community of real people who were facing the same dilemmas as Sonya and I. One father opened up about his family's desperate need for respite from caring for their ten-year-old. Another mother was puzzled about why her little girl violently resisted getting a haircut. Some parents talked about the difficulties in getting other family members to understand their son or daughter was not going to "just grow out of" his or her behaviors. There were parents who, just like me, were online conducting their own uncharted search for a treatment for their child. Coming across these accounts moved me enormously and marked one of the first times I felt as though we were not alone.

However with this relief came disappointment, because no one offered stories of recovery. A few basic themes prevailed. The first was since no two children are alike, no two treatment regimens would be the same. The second was, no one, including the medical community, is certain what causes autism. The third was, parents must research, consult with professionals, and figure out for themselves what they think will help their child. Another was, most forms of treatment are very expensive and not likely covered by insurance.

One breakthrough came when my online research led to a recommendation to try a casein-free diet, a popular dietary intervention for autism involving removing dairy and any other foods containing milk protein from the child's diet. Many parents reported their autistic children's behavior improved significantly after putting them on a casein-free diet, and a woman from my church whose two sons were on the autism spectrum told me she had experienced similar results within a short period of time

The diet itself seemed straightforward and not very difficult to implement, so we went for it. The result was an immediate difference in Matthew's behavior. He was not perfectly calm, but he became noticeably less hyper. We were amazed something so simple could have such tremendous results. It was our first experience seeing Matthew's behavior change based on something concrete that we were able to do ourselves.

The majority of the books and journals I read indicated there was no known cure for autistic behaviors—only treatments that could help children on the spectrum improve. However, a couple of books and a lot of web content from independent researchers claimed, in some instances, full recovery from autism was possible, and it was taking place. It was clear that getting Matthew healthy would not involve traditional medical methods. Autism seemed elusive. It was like a thief who somehow crept into a tightly locked house under moonlight, ransacked the house, and made a clean getaway. In the morning, the homeowner clearly sees evidence they were robbed, but no clues were left to track down the thief. And, in the case of autism, even if a cause could be found, there was still no cure waiting in the wings—or was there?

BIOMEDICAL INTERVENTIONS

ON FRIDAY, NOVEMBER 16, 2007, I was working from my basement office as usual. Sonya had already gone to pick up Matthew from school, and the house was quiet except for the faint sound of the television on the floor above me. I finished a conference call and took a walk upstairs to stretch my legs. As I reached the top of the stairs and entered the living room, the TV caught my attention. It was tuned to a popular talk show, and the guests were a doctor and two women with a child. They were talking about autism, which, as always when I saw anything pertaining to autism, stopped me in my tracks and grabbed all of my attention. The doctor was reporting that, in some instances, children can be completely healed of autism through a physiological approach, which he referred to as biomedical interventions.

My heart skipped a beat as I tried to pick up the thread in the middle of the interview. I gathered that both of the women were mothers of an autistic child, and one was crying because she was at her wits' end. After taking her son to numerous physicians, she had lost all hope he would someday get well. The doctor consoled her and assured her that he could help her son. His name was Dr. Thomas Samuels, MD.

I was mesmerized. The host asked the doctor whether or not autism was a permanent and irreversible condition, and he replied in no uncertain terms that he had helped many children get better or even recover completely. I hurried into the kitchen and fumbled through drawers to find a pen and paper so I could write down his name, all while trying not to miss a word.

For the next three hours, I kept dissecting the doctor's

comments and analyzing the credibility of the show, trying to figure out if the episode could be a hoax. The host was one of the more reputable daytime personalities, and I could not imagine the show's guests were less than credible; however, hearing someone claim on national television that symptoms of autism could be reversed seemed like a dream. It was one thing to read such a claim on the web, where people could hide behind their computers and servers, but it was another to hear it firsthand from a doctor who was staking his reputation on it.

Later that afternoon, when Sonya came home with Matthew, I could hardly contain myself. I showed her the doctor's name on the scrap of paper I was holding and babbled almost incoherently about what I'd just seen and heard. I felt like someone who had just won a sweepstakes. I finally managed to get across what the doctor on television had said, and Sonya asked if I thought we should take Matthew to see him.

The doctor's office was eight hundred miles away, and, in spite of my excitement, I felt apprehensive about saying yes. I still wondered if the program might have been some sort of drama that was made for television. "What if it doesn't work?" I asked myself. But I decided getting Matthew well was worth the risk, and I told Sonya I thought we should go.

A week later, after reviewing the doctor's Web site, I called his office and set up an appointment for four months out, which was the first date available. We could not see the doctor who was on television, but instead our appointment was with his colleague, Dr. Ronald Jackson, who practiced in the same office. The wait to see Dr. Samuels, who was world-renowned, was much longer than four months.

We booked airline tickets, made hotel reservations, and planned to stay for three days near Dr. Jackson's office in Connecticut. The appointment would only take one day, but it was our first time flying with Matthew and Jaida, and we wanted to travel without pressure on the day before and after

Matthew's appointment. We also hoped to have a little fun while we were away.

In preparation for the appointment, I read Dr. Jackson's book about the rise, in recent years, of autism in children. It outlined the history of autism, the leading theories about its cause, and his approach to treating autistic children. I dove in feverishly, and I was moved by the stories about the different children he and his colleagues had treated and his honesty about the varying degrees of success they'd achieved.

I also found the book fascinating from a completely biological standpoint. Dr. Jackson used comparisons between symptoms of autism and similar symptoms of other treatable children's illnesses as a basis to look for potentially effective therapies. As far as I knew, there was a lot of research supporting Dr. Jackson's work, but it was not as recognized as other treatments, such as Applied Behavior Analysis (ABA). In my opinion, this was because ABA had much more documented evidence proving its effectiveness.

As I read, I saw our family's story reflected in the book's first few chapters describing not only the children's illnesses, but also the hardships endured by the parents and families who cared for them. It was clear from Dr. Jackson's writing that he was not only a leader in his field, but he genuinely cared about all aspects of his area of expertise. The book went into great detail about different treatments, starting with fairly simple approaches, such as food allergy testing, food elimination, and special diets; and, moving on to nutritional supplementation, detoxification, and medication.

I don't know if I was just desperate for an answer or if Dr. Jackson's approach appealed to my sense of logic, but his reputation, detailed description of his research, and pragmatic approach to healing convinced me he could, and would, heal Matthew. He discussed symptoms I saw in Matthew, and he related them to possible causes and treatments. He admitted that healing could take years, and not all children are good candidates for complete healing, though many could make notable progress. I decided beforehand, come what may, we were going to stick with the treatment until Matthew got well—no matter what.

SETTING OUR SIGHTS ON RECOVERY

MARCH 2008 MARKED the beginning of a new stage in all of our lives. It represented a significant change in what we were doing to bolster Matthew's growth and to improve his quality of life. Our understanding of autism and our hopes for Matthew's recovery would increase drastically in the upcoming months, but so would something else we thought had already reached its limit—our fatigue and stress levels.

On March 4, our family took a surprisingly smooth four-hour flight from Atlanta to Connecticut. As we left Atlanta's Hartsfield-Jackson Airport, Matthew was as curious as ever, and Jaida, only nine months old, snuggled against Sonya in a baby sling.

In planning for the flight, Sonya and I had hoped for the best, but prepared for the worst, so we brought toys to keep Matthew occupied. We had heard horror stories about special-needs children having a hard time traveling by plane. We did not think Matthew would have a problem once we were airborne, but we were concerned he might have trouble during takeoff and landing if he felt pressure in his ears. Thankfully, that did not happen and our flight was pretty uneventful.

Connecticut was cold and there was snow on the ground. The sky was stone gray, and it was sleeting sporadically. We picked up our rental car and drove forty-five minutes on slushy highways. When we reached our destination, we were pleasantly surprised to find the town was less remote than our research had led us to expect. The hotel was new and modern, and we were minutes from a shopping mall and restaurants, giving us one less logistical detail to worry about. It was nice to be away from home, even if the reason for our trip weighed heavily on our minds.

That evening, we relaxed in our room and enjoyed the hotel's swimming pool before calling it a night. We wanted to get a good night's rest because the next day would start early, and it would be a big day for all of us. Our minds were rational and calm, but our hearts were brimming over with nervous hope for the impossible. Sonya and I knew Dr. Jackson could not make any promises, but we were yearning for good news, even if it were just that Matthew seemed like a likely candidate for improvement—anything that would indicate he might have a brighter future.

The following day our family arrived at Dr. Jackson's office ten minutes late for our 8:30 AM appointment, but other than having difficulty following the driving directions, the morning went smoothly. We were not allowed to give Matthew anything to eat or drink from the time he went to bed the night before until the completion of blood tests that morning, so we were anxious not to delay the process. By the time we arrived, Matthew was doing pretty well, but it pained us not to be able to feed him, and we knew in a little while, he would react to his hunger.

Dr. Jackson's practice was located thirty minutes from the hotel, in a quiet, old town whose winding roads and cozy ambiance made it look like something out of a movie. The office was an old, three-story house with winding staircases, and was under renovation. We'd sent most of our paperwork in advance, so we only had to fill out something called a "behavioral checklist," which identified common autistic traits (e.g., tantrums or resistance to schedule changes), before seeing the doctor.

The receptionist, a friendly woman in her fifties, obviously had many irons in the fire, which was not surprising. Since we had to schedule our appointment so far in advance, we knew the practice's services were in demand by many families like ours. The growth of the special-needs culture to which we belonged was emphasized when I was parking the car minutes earlier. The man in the parking spot to the left of mine was getting out of his car with his son. He looked at our license plate, smiled, and said, "So, you came all the way from North Carolina too?" We were actually from Georgia, and the car was rented, but his sentiment was appreciated. We both desperately wanted to alleviate our children's pain.

The receptionist did not take any insurance information because the office only accepted insurance on a very limited basis; instead, they provided us with receipts so we could deal directly with our insurance company. This was probably because they specialized in health issues generally not considered treatable, aside from prescribing a couple of approved drugs. I assumed it would make for a real claims nightmare later on. At the moment, we were paying by credit card, and we were not sure exactly how much the tests would cost.

We waited for about fifteen minutes before being called up to the second floor where Matthew's basic physical information—height, weight, temperature, and blood pressure—was taken. The examination rooms were small and confining. Though Matthew fidgeted a lot, considering he had not eaten in twelve hours and had slept in a strange bed the night before, he was pretty responsive and well behaved.

In a patient room around the corner, Sonya and I could hear a distraught, adolescent girl crying as she resisted some type of procedure. Matthew did not seem to notice, though it distracted Sonya and me until I caught sight of Dr. Samuels walking past us and into his office. I poked Sonya, trying not to be too obvious, and said. "There's Dr. Samuels. He's the one I saw on TV." "I know," Sonya said calmly and discreetly. I was suddenly struck with the enormity of traveling eight hundred miles to see a doctor.

Before we knew it, we were with Dr. Jackson. His cramped office held just his desk, a couple of guest chairs, and some wooden bookshelves. By now, Matthew was hungry and antsy. The combination of trying to pacify him and manage our own concern about his discomfort made it difficult for us to focus on what Dr. Jackson was saying, so Sonya and I took turns listening closely and attending to Matthew. After a long string of questions, Dr. Jackson began to provide some feedback. He was calm, professional, and respectful.

"I haven't heard anything in your responses that sounds really remarkable—meaning Paul Jr. is symptomatically similar to a lot of children we see. Are you familiar with what we do?"

"We've read your book," I said.

"Ok, so then you understand how we approach treatment?" he asked.

"Yes. I mean, we made the decision to travel eight hundred miles. So we had a pretty good idea of what we were coming for."

"Good. That gives me a good feel for how much background I need to try to explain, apart from the specific treatments we will try." He then went on to describe the first steps he had in mind, starting immediately with vitamin B-12 supplements and a special diet.

From Dr. Jackson's office, we proceeded to another examination room to have Matthew's blood drawn to test for comprehensive allergies, toxins, and traces of anything else known to produce the type of delays he was experiencing. But first, we had to speak with the practice's financial manager to discuss the cost of the testing. We were not prepared for what ensued.

Sonya and I had set aside money for the visit. We were living paycheck to paycheck with just a little going into savings each month, and our savings account was not sufficient to cover the tests. Though the financial manager was not pushy, I felt anxious. Matthew was starving and no longer able to manage himself. If he could speak, he would have told us that his stomach and possibly his head were hurting. We had food for him in our bag, and it took everything in me not to break it out and feed him.

I broke out into a sweat trying to figure out how we were going to pay $1800 more than the $2000 we had available, in addition to the $1000 we had spent in travel costs. Sonya was occupied with feeding Jaida, while Matthew was one-step short of sobbing in despair. I was overwhelmed with trying to balance our bank account from memory and figuring out what was available on our credit cards. We had traveled so far, but, without prepayment, the tests could not be performed.

As uncomfortable and slightly embarrassing as it was, I told the finance manager that Sonya and I needed to take a second to discuss the matter privately. She seemed to understand, and I got the impression she had received this request many times before. I was pretty sure we did not have enough money available on our credit cards, and the only thing I had with me was a charge card, which we'd sworn never to use unless we had a *true emergency*; I did not think paying for these services qualified as one.

We found a spot on a small bench in the unpainted alcove near the staircase, stretching our legs from the bench seat to the wall in order to prevent Matthew from running out of the tiny nook. He was irritated, distressed, and restless, and he kept asking for food. It was a relief not to have to work out our situation in front of a stranger anymore, but I still felt the pressure of having to make a quick decision. We did not travel this far *not* to do everything the doctor was prescribing. So, we talked through how to pay off the emergency-card balance when we got home, and we decided to use it to pay the additional $1800.

In order to ease the burden on patients like us, Dr. Jackson sent only the highly specialized tests to the labs he used. He gave us a prescription for the more routine testing that we could take to Matthew's regular pediatrician, who would then draw blood and have it analyzed under our regular health insurance. A nurse walked us through everything that was not carried out that morning.

After a nurse drew blood from Matthew, he received his first dose of vitamin B-12 on the spot. When she explained to us that the shot would be given by needle, we felt badly for Matthew. When she added that he would get this shot every three days, and we would be the ones who gave it to him, we felt badly for ourselves. Our worries lessened as she explained that children often got the shot while they were sleeping, so they were less aware of the needle's pinch. Sonya still had some objections, and I was concerned, but we wanted to do whatever was necessary in order to get Matthew better.

The nurse explained how to give the shot and then demonstrated it on Matthew. I held him and tried to quiet him while she pinched a small area of his bottom, quickly inserted the needle, and pressed the top of the syringe with her thumb. Predictably, Matthew cried at the top of his lungs, and we felt horribly again. In reality, the shot probably felt like nothing more than a tiny sting, but he was already traumatized. He hadn't eaten, he was in a strange place, and he had spent the morning being examined and stuck with needles by strangers.

Sonya and I felt really sorry for Matthew. Prior to the shot, he had seven vials of blood drawn. Over the past nine months, Matthew had been poked and prodded by doctors enough to know he hated it. He had gotten to the point he would start to cry whenever we even pulled up outside of his regular pediatrician's office. Thankfully, this shot was administered relatively quickly, and he settled down once we gave him an apple, which he ate as if it were the last one on earth.

Four hours had passed while we were at Dr. Jackson's office, and we knew it had been a difficult time for Matthew and Jaida because we felt drained ourselves. We were as relieved as Matthew that it was over. We agreed we would begin the treatments Dr. Jackson prescribed, and then schedule a follow-up phone call with him in five to six weeks to discuss how Matthew was doing and to determine the next steps. It was now about 1:00 PM and we had the rest of the day to ourselves. We were eager to counter the morning's nerve-racking experience with something more pleasant.

The curving, wet roads were less unnerving driving out of the little, historic town than they were driving into it. The shoulders were covered in mounds of snow, which was tainted gray by traffic, but we passed a fenced-in playground where the snow was still pure white. There was not much else to see, but we were happy. Now that the doctor's appointment was over, we felt a sense of accomplishment similar to finishing a difficult footrace. We were doing our best for Matthew, and we had never expected it to be easy. We were thankful we had risen to the challenge. Best of all, we were together and not in a rush.

As we neared the highway leading back to the hotel, we passed a small lake edged with tall, snow-covered trees, which was a far cry from the scenery we left in Georgia a day ago. It made us feel as if we were really away, and, for a second I pretended we were in some exotic place, and the trip was purely for leisure. As usual, Matthew stared out of the back window, and Jaida slept in her car seat.

As Sonya and I drove along, discussing our impressions of Matthew's appointment, the morning's tension finally began to leave our shoulders. We ate lunch at a family restaurant, and the kids enjoyed it. We did too. We took our time getting back to the hotel where Sonya and Jaida got some rest while I took Matthew swimming.

The next morning, we left Connecticut bright and early to return to Atlanta. In spite of our concern about the cost of future appointments and services, we were glad we had made the trip. Our up-and-down ride between optimism and despair was on the upside, and we felt good about giving Matthew the best chance possible. We hoped we were not setting ourselves up for a huge letdown.

THERAPIES AND TREATMENTS

LATE ONE WEEKNIGHT, sometime after 10:00 PM I was cleaning instead of getting ready for bed. I could not resist the urge to move an old personal computer from the closet in our master bathroom down to the basement. Suddenly I remembered that I had video footage of Matthew as a newborn saved on the computer's hard drive.

I had recently been trying to figure out exactly when we started to notice Matthew's delays, such as when he stopped making eye contact with us, which is a typical, autistic spectrum disorder trait. It seemed to me he had not always shown developmental delays, and, if I could figure out when they started, I might be able to pinpoint some trigger. Like most people in adverse situations, I wanted to know why ours had occurred. Deep in my heart, I had always wondered whether antibiotics or even the vaccinations he received as a four-pound baby played any part in his illness.

With some effort, I managed to track down the videos on the old hard drive, and I found myself watching a three-month-old Matthew on the screen. He was tiny and frail, but very attentive. As I moved from left to right with the camera, his eyes followed me closely. It was radically different from his current lack of eye contact.

During Matthew's appointment in Connecticut, we told Dr. Jackson that Matthew appeared to have regressed in his development. This was significant because autistic children who had experienced regression were more likely to reach full recovery than those who did not. The video confirmed our assessment was accurate. Matthew had physical limitations in the womb that could have contributed to any number of his issues, but we had definitely observed the disappearance of early speech, social awareness, and eye contact; therefore, he could feasibly be a candidate for full recovery.

I hoped some weird toxin, vitamin deficiency, or allergy would show up in the blood tests taken at Dr. Jackson's office that would provide a clue about his condition. Any of these things would take some time to correct, but Matthew would still have great promise for a full recovery. I had heard, in some cases, the proper biological treatment, combined with occupational or speech therapy to make up for the lapse during which they could not properly receive cognitive input, could, within months, transform an autistic child into a typically developing kid.

Watching the video, my optimistic nature won out over my more practical side, which kept saying Matthew's growth would be a long, slow process. I found myself daydreaming about the day I would call my family and friends to tell them Matthew no longer had autism!

Upon request, we had a copy of the blood test results mailed to our home. I would have considered it good news to find out his tests revealed high traces of lead or some other toxic metal because it would at least give us something identifiable. But my hopes were deflated. Other than one major food allergy and a few vitamin deficiencies, there were no such results from any of his blood work. This meant there would be no change to Dr. Jackson's prescribed course of dietary modifications and supplements.

VITAMIN B-12

ON MARCH 14, a blue and white USPS box was left on our front step. It came from a compound pharmacy in Secaucus, New Jersey and contained a month's supply of methyl B-12 vitamin shots packed in ice in a Styrofoam box. Though I was happy it came, I was nervous about administering the shot to Matthew.

The primary purpose of B-12 was to help Matthew's body remove toxins by natural means, such as perspiration or waste elimination. If we were lucky, it would also help him sleep; if we were unlucky, the dose would be too high and cause him to be aggressive or overly emotional.

We decided giving Matthew the shot at night would be best, so I waited until 11:30 PM when he was in a deep sleep. I was nervous. The needle was so tiny that I feared it might break when I tried to insert it into his skin. In a jittery state, on my first try, I accidentally ejected all the fluid from the syringe into the air. The crimson fluid catapulted out, splattering the carpet and the corner of Matthew's mattress. This mishap created a dilemma, because the supply was calibrated so Matthew would receive one syringe every four days, starting with the lowest of three doses and working up.

Dr. Jackson's instructions were to observe Matthew's reaction to each injection over a four-day period to see whether a dose was too strong or too weak. After we determined which dose he tolerated best, we were then supposed to switch from giving him shots every four days to every three days. Now, we would have to begin with the second dose.

I hurried downstairs to the refrigerator to get another syringe, and I returned on tiptoe into Matthew's bedroom. He was asleep on his stomach, and I carefully pulled his pajamas down to expose a small section of his bottom. I tried to recall exactly what the nurse at the doctor's office had done. I wanted to give it to him as quickly as she did so there would be little chance of waking him up.

As I lowered the tip of the needle toward Matthew, cradling the B-12 shot between my index and middle fingers, I paused. Matthew was the most handsome little boy I had ever seen. He had extra-long, curly eyelashes, which looked beautiful against the light bronze skin of his face. I loved to watch him sleep. It was one of the few times when he looked like any other child and I felt like any other dad—absent of worry about whether or not he would progress. In moments like those, I daydreamed again about the type of person I hoped Matthew would be when he grew up: compassionate, strong, and a great motivator who loved God and helped people.

Turning my attention back to the B-12 shot, I reached down, squeezed a small, fatty spot of his bottom and inserted the needle. I pressed the syringe with my thumb, and the contents exited the plastic tube and vanished into Matthew's body. He flinched a little and sat up to see what had stung him. I hid the needle behind my back and switched off the light. Matthew returned to a hard, fast sleep as quickly as he had sat up. I was relieved it was over.

This routine took place every three nights for the next year and a half, no matter what. If I was tired, he got a shot. If we were on vacation, he got a shot. If he was tired, he got a shot. If we had some big event, he got a shot. Every now and again I would spill one, but, for the most part, it went pretty smoothly. We had to alternate each shot from the left side of his bottom to the right. We started a log to keep track, and to note his progress.

We called Dr. Jackson's office for occasional clarifications or questions, but, over time, I became increasingly comfortable giving Matthew his shot. Unfortunately, Matthew became more and more fearful of it. It did not seem to hurt too much—he whined more than cried—but he just did not like it, which we found perfectly legitimate.

Throughout April, the benefits of the shots were close to what we had expected. Methyl B-12 was intended to help him detoxify, and, while there was no way for us to visibly tell whether or not this was happening, I did notice he began to sweat more, which is one way the body releases toxins. Matthew had rarely sweated prior to the injections, no matter how active or hot he was. We understood very little about the biological aspect of it all, but we were sure this changed after a couple of months on the supplements.

The greatest immediate result was that Matthew began to go to sleep earlier and even sleep through the night. Previously, in addition to regularly waking up around 3:00 AM and not going back to sleep, he also had difficulty falling asleep every night at bedtime. Once Matthew started on B-12, it took him much less time to fall asleep. Not only could his body now get a decent amount of rest, but also Sonya and I could start to catch up on our sleep as well.

There had been many mornings in the past when we did not want to wake Matthew up and drive him to school because he had just fallen asleep. Staff at the early intervention program advised us to bring him to school no matter what. They were experienced working with children who had sleep issues, and they felt if Matthew were awakened after a night of little sleep, he would end up tired enough to sleep the next night. Also, they believed he would realize, even if he did not sleep, he still had to go to school, so he would be motivated to sleep. They were so sure that they allowed him to arrive at school in his pajamas, if necessary, and dressed him later.

The advice seemed logical enough, but it was hard to execute. Matthew contracted strep throat almost every month, and we were sure his immune system was weak. We knew his mind and body needed more rest than he was getting, and we felt as if we were mistreating him by forcing him to get up and go to school when he had just fallen asleep an hour earlier. On the other hand, we also knew he needed the daily therapy provided by the school. Sonya and I decided, if he were tired, we would take him to school no matter what, but if he were getting sick, we would not. The methyl B-12 supplements went a long way in alleviating this problem.

On the down side, we saw our laid-back, mild-mannered child become more aggressive. Matthew never had tantrums before, but as soon as he started taking the supplements, he began to have episodes when he would gnash his teeth or grab our clothing and stamp his feet. Sometimes, he would have angry outbursts, yelling and banging his hands repeatedly over his head. It was our impression he was frustrated or hurting, and he desperately wanted to communicate this. This happened too frequently for us to take it lightly.

Matthew also became more emotional. It was tough to see him cry for no apparent reason, bury his face in his hands, or just seem sad. We even considered stopping the supplement, but we decided the pros outweighed the cons.

Matthew's aggressive behavior eventually became a daily occurrence at home, although we received no bad school reports. On one of our phone appointments with Dr. Jackson, we mentioned this to him, and he decreased the dosage. Matthew's aggression waned, but he still had emotional outbursts and moments of sadness.

From a financial standpoint, the B-12 supplement added another one hundred dollars a month to our already stretched budget. Occasionally, we paid the pharmacy in cash, and every so often we put the bill on our credit card. We felt that any treatment was worth the cost, if only to identify what was effective and what was not. Matthew was now four and a half years old, and we remained hopeful about his future. The task at hand was to be patient and stay the course. On April 24, 2008, I wrote the following in our journal:

Matthew fell asleep last night (about midnight). He was really aggressive when he got home from school today. He slept all the way on the ride home, which means that he was extremely tired. I put him to bed early tonight and he fell asleep around 9:00 PM. He slept through the entire night. We received the lower dosage of B-12 today from the pharmacy in New Jersey. Some clearer speech at this point, but progress is still slow moving. Matthew is learning to swim and not at all afraid of the water. He can now count to twenty and identify the numbers. He is smart. He loves the playground and outdoors in general.

GOOD NUTRITION

FOR TWO YEARS, we carefully monitored everything Matthew ate. We were now in the process of cautiously introducing new foods to try to figure out what was good for him and what was not, which foods seemed to help him maintain self-control, and which ones exacerbated his autistic behaviors. With the simultaneous introduction of supplements, it was hard to know what contributed to a positive or negative change in his behavior, but when we had a hunch that a certain food was harmful, we allowed him to eat it for a specific period and monitored his behavior. In no sense did we have this down to a science; often, we just followed our parental intuition.

Beyond just trying to take care of Matthew's immediate needs, I was inclined to avoid giving our kids foods containing a lot of sugar or high-fructose corn syrup so they would not fall into a habit of eating fast foods and sweets instead of more nutritious foods. There was a lot of publicly available health information indicating obesity and diabetes were up among children due, in part, to poor eating habits.

Sonya did not always share my zealousness for cutting out all foods containing ingredients that were less than wholesome. But our differing opinions had the advantage of providing us with some balance, and Sonya kept me from inadvertently doing things like spoiling Matthew's fun on holidays. Although he could be a picky eater, he loved green vegetables, so getting him to eat healthy was already fairly easy. Sonya reminded me that life would not come to a screeching halt if he deviated from the ideal once in a while.

We did try to feed Matthew as little processed food as possible. My research had left me apprehensive about putting anything into Matthew's body his blood tests indicated that he was allergic to—no matter how small the reaction—or that contained any unnatural ingredients, such as dyes and preservatives. I discovered that processed foods make up the bulk of what's found on grocery store shelves and the bulk of what's consumed within our society, which makes it hard to find a solid variety of foods for Matthew. We spent a lot of time and money in very few grocery stores.

In order to minimize pesticides and maximize nutrients, we decided to feed Matthew as much organic food as possible, including as much organic meat as we could afford. Because it isn't mass-produced and is raised and grown in a way that usually incurs more costs, organic meat and produce is typically much more expensive than the conventional foods sold in large supermarkets.

By the middle of March 2008, Matthew's regular diet consisted primarily of: sweet potatoes, organic brown rice, organic cabbage, organic chicken, brown rice pasta, organic string beans, plain potato chips, corn chips, peas, uncured organic chicken, turkey hot dogs, uncured chicken sausage, pork chops, steak, black-eyed peas, spinach, gluten-free bologna, gluten-free cereal, soy milk, collard and mustard greens, and organic applesauce.

We were always seeking to increase his intake of nutrient-filled foods, but we also had to stay away from any foods provoking any kind of visible reaction. For example, nonorganic garlic, seafood, and certain other foods tended to give him a rash on his face. It was a tough regimen to stick to at times, but our reward was the satisfaction of knowing we were doing all we could to help our son, and we were not giving him food detrimental to his growth and well-being.

FOOD ELIMINATION AND SPECIAL DIETS

WHEN I FIRST read an online list of available gluten-free foods, I wondered how anybody could possibly feed their child from the narrow selection. Cashew butter? Almond milk? I was sure it would be impossible to get Matthew to eat the options I was finding, He was a kid, after all, not an adult who could understand and then will himself to eat right. The gluten-free recipes I found seemed more like strange concoctions than healthy meals and treats. Rice meatballs? Soy soup? I was not inspired, and I did not think Matthew would be either.

During our visit with Dr. Jackson, we had agreed to try a gluten-free diet on Matthew. Gluten is a protein found in wheat, barley, and some other grains that contain a component thought to cause damage in the small intestines of some people. I had heard the diet produced positive results in 60 percent of the autistic children who tried it, and, though these numbers were based on a small population, many parents and practitioners agreed the diet had a lot of potential to improve autistic children's behaviors.

Though I did not fully grasp the biology behind gluten

sensitivity, one thing I knew was the diet had to be followed strictly or it would not work. Even the smallest amount of gluten in Matthew's diet would negate any potential benefits, which made it difficult on many levels. For one thing, Sonya and I differed on the importance of this diet. She thought it seemed harsh, especially since Matthew's diet was already so restricted and he weighed less than the average child his age. She felt he needed to eat more foods, not less, and cutting out foods he was willing to eat was not in his best interest.

Also, Sonya legitimately felt implementing a gluten-free regimen was a lot to put Matthew and us through when there was no guarantee it would help him. I agreed that it was a lot to endure, but I was willing to try anything that might help. Dr. Jackson had asked us to try this diet for a minimum of three months in conjunction with the other treatments. Stopping before the end of that period could distort our observations of Matthew's progress. Sonya and I disagreed strongly. At the time, I did most of the grocery shopping, and I read every label before I would allow any food to cross our threshold. I prepared special meals for Matthew, and even then I sometimes felt I was not doing enough; I came across one suggestion that following the diet correctly required cooking the food in specially designated pots and pans. We never went that far, but I never stopped wondering if we should have.

The emotional element, on top of the existing daily stress, sometimes caused conflict between Sonya and me because, subtly, I placed the burden I felt to *fix* Matthew, on her.

"Matthew is already being stuck with needles every three days and is not allowed to eat anything that tastes good to him," she said, irritated by my insistence that we be more strict with his diet. "We are doing as much as we can. Matthew will start taking five or six supplements by mouth every day. We will have to give them to him at scheduled times every day. We are driving four hours every day with him in a car seat to get to the New Center. He is a boy, Paul, not an experiment; we are parents, not medical researchers. I want his home to be a place for him to feel loved and encouraged and have fun, not a hospital."

I did not know what to say. I could feel again, not only was I pushing myself, but I was pushing Sonya as well. I knew her sentiment was correct in many ways, and my intensity was due partly to my fear that someday I would not be able to tell Matthew with a clear conscience I did everything I could to help him. I also still had my eye on the trophy I called "full recovery," and I was willing to do anything to get it. I wanted to offer Sonya some mental relief by telling her we could ease up on the gluten-free diet, but my passionate all-in-or-all-out personality would not let me. I was not there yet. Instead, I told her, "I'll do all the diet stuff and handle all his meals, so you won't have to deal with it."

As the months went by, we saw no benefits from Matthew's gluten-free diet. In the back of my mind, I wondered if the diet might not have worked because I was not strict enough. I thought about birthday parties where Matthew snatched cake and ice cream from someone else's dish or ate fast food when we were unprepared on a road trip.

In general, I remained reluctant to let him eat a crumb of anything I had the slightest notion might be bad for him, and I monitored his behavior for weeks after giving him anything new. The problem with this was that with so many variables that could impact his behavior—everything from sleep, to his daily activities, to a new song he heard and recited in his mind all day—it was rarely possible to know what really influenced his behavior on any particular day. Only once or twice did I ever put my finger on something that had an adverse effect on his conduct, and the evidence in those cases was pure observation. Over time, I remained hesitant about letting Matthew eat certain foods, and Sonya continued to try to help me relax and trust God more than my own efforts.

RESTRICTING TOXINS

SOME MEDICAL PROFESSIONALS believe that if toxins build up in the body, they can negatively affect routine bodily functions. The human body is designed to rid itself of unwanted substances through waste elimination, perspiring, and healthy immune activity. This is its way of fighting off the barrage of germs and other contaminants resulting from exposure to pollution, dirt, pesticides, and other natural and unnatural conditions. Since we noticed Matthew did not sweat much prior to taking vitamin B-12 and discovered that many autistic children's bodies did not properly detoxify, we wondered if this might have been an ongoing problem for him.

We had already been doing our best to reduce Matthew's intake of harmful substances by feeding him only organic foods. We were happy to discover this was an important step in the right direction. The safety of pesticide levels on supermarket produce is a controversial subject. Some regulatory agencies claim that the amount of pesticides ingested by people who eat typical grocery store produce is completely safe. However, there is also a pool of research claiming current pesticide levels can be linked to certain types of cancer, attention disorders in children, weak immune systems, and other health problems.

It became important to ask questions routinely about our family's food. For produce, the question was, "How and where was it grown, and how was it transported to my supermarket?" For all other processed foods, the question was, "What is in it?" I began to buy as much food as possible that did not contain dyes, preservatives, or ingredient names too long for me to pronounce.

We also avoided genetically modified foods, which are foods whose original structure had been altered through genetic engineering. The purpose of genetic engineering is usually to produce a specific quality, such as increased amounts of a certain nutrient or a longer shelf life. I never came across any proof that genetically modified foods were unsafe, but the public controversy about their potential health risks led me to cross them off my shopping list. Since genetically modified foods are not legally required to be labeled as such in the United States, buying organic had the added advantage of ensuring Matthew was not exposed to them.

As I worked on Matthew's diet, I became aware of a growing movement among parents around the country who were going completely Green, ridding their homes of household cleaners, cosmetics, laundry soaps, and other domestic products that might expose their children to harmful chemicals. Our search for healthy practices that might aid Matthew's progress did not quite lead us down that road; we left it as an area to explore further later on.

SUPPLEMENTATION

BY LATE SPRING 2008, we had added more supplements to Matthew's regimen, including biotin, omega fish oil, vitamin E, and phosphate. Some he received in the morning, and some in the evening. Some were to be administered with food, others without. Some were a half teaspoon, and some were a full teaspoon. We often forgot which was which and had to refer to notes in our daily log.

We definitely saw benefits. Prior to taking the supplements, Matthew was often sick with cold and flu symptoms, and was especially prone to getting a cough that would last for weeks. He rarely, if ever, got over an illness without an antibiotic. But, after we started him on the supplements, it was like a small miracle to see him recover from illnesses on the strength of his own immune system. Sonya and I were ecstatic.

Matthew began to seem cognitively clearer, pronouncing words more coherently; though there was no definitive way to attribute it to the supplements or to nutrition. However, he also began to gain weight, and we were sure this was a result of the vitamins. Prior to that point, his weight had not gone up one pound in over a year.

Nonetheless, other areas remained unchanged. His attention span, which was of vital importance to us, did not improve. His daily behavior reports from school reflected he still had a hard time focusing, and we saw the same thing at home. Sometimes he loved nothing better than to run around in circles, and he usually had a hard time staying on a task unless it was something he was compulsively interested in. At night, before going to bed, it was a struggle to get him to settle down. Often, we just let him roll around in bed yelling or laughing hysterically until he got so tired that he fell asleep. Some nights, we had to screw the light bulbs out of the sockets in his room because he would turn the light on in the middle of the night and climb up in the windowsill. We did not really care what neighbors thought, but, from a standpoint of safety and security, it was scary.

Even with the additional supplements, Matthew appeared to engage even more in self-soothing behaviors, such as stimming and putting his hand or other objects in his mouth. This was no indication he was not still improving, but a positive change in this area might have indicated progress by leaps and bounds as opposed to slow and steady growth. Nevertheless, we celebrated any victory no matter how small, whether it was in his language, social development, or general health. We were settling deeper into accepting years could pass before we saw Matthew really grow in the way we believed he could and would. We kept in mind that healing was what we were after, and we were taking solid steps toward it. The growth we were hoping for began way below the surface.

Financially, we continued to devise ways to pay for supplements from month to month. We were starting to rob Peter to pay Paul in our budget, and we just kept improvising. When we charged supplements on our credit card, we knew we would not be able to pay it off at the end of the billing cycle. We were living beyond what we could afford, but we felt Matthew needed, and clearly benefited from, what we were doing. On nights when Sonya and I were so tired that we felt we could not muster the energy to measure out supplements, or get up at midnight to give Matthew a B-12 shot, and questioned if what we were doing was worth the effort and costs, we focused on the visible results, such as Matthew's weight gain and his stronger immune response.

GASTROINTESTINAL ISSUES

I WATCHED AS Matthew played on the other side of the room. Near him, Jaida was lying on a blanket on the couch. Every now and then, I would catch a look in his eye or something in his behavior that gave the appearance of a very capable child who was trapped by an anatomy not yet prepared for all he wanted to do. His eyes were glazed over, as if intoxicated, yet he seemed to be only a breath away from conversing and sharing his thoughts just like anybody else.

Dr. Jackson had mentioned, even though Matthew's tests did not reveal any gastrointestinal issues, a child's behavior was sometimes a better indicator of that type of problem than was the test. I suspected this might be the case with Matthew.

We continued to have phone appointments with Dr. Jackson every other month, and, during the next one, I shared my suspicions with him. He ordered a heavy metals DMSA (dimercaptosuccinic acid) challenge test, which involves testing a urine sample following the ingestion of a drug that attaches to heavy metals in the body and draws them out during urination. It was a more accurate way to check Matthew's body for the presence of toxic metals than were his earlier blood tests, which had come up negative. However, it was considered a dangerous procedure—one that some doctors who treated people with autism did not approve of.

Sonya and I spent a great deal of time discussing whether or not we should go through with it, finally deciding to go ahead. The test results came back negative. Dr. Jackson then ordered an antifungal medication to address the possible overgrowth of fungus that could cause digestive problems and contribute to toxicity. This also produced no results and revealed no treatable issues. The disappointment was like déjà vu, yet I knew things would be better in the future.

The DMSA-challenge procedure and antifungal medication required more money and more time and resulted in little more than the peace of mind we got from ruling out another potential cause for Matthew's behaviors and delays. But in the end, we felt it was worth it. Some families had great success after identifying what was going on in their children's guts, and it would have driven me crazy to leave that stone unturned. We were pushing ahead on his road to recovery.

MEDICATION

ONE OF MY underlying objectives in our approach to treatment was to avoid, at all costs, putting Matthew on medication—especially before he could talk and tell us how it made him feel. Sonya was more open to it than I was because she believed Attention Deficit Disorder (ADD) medication might help Matthew get the most out of the input he was receiving in his early intervention program. The result could be increased knowledge and corrected behavior. I knew there was a lot of validity to that line of thinking, but I was skeptical about the prevalent use of ADD medications among children in American society. To me, it seemed like an attempt to treat children's symptoms rather than addressing the underlying causes of their disorders and healing them.

I had long suspected prescription medications partly benefited the health of the public, and partly benefited the bottom lines of the companies that manufactured them. After years of reading, listening to natural health radio shows, and talking with friends in the medical profession about the benefits of nutrition and a preventative approach to maintaining good health, I was not eager to accept pharmaceuticals as the best approach to common, and sometimes uncommon, medical issues.

I was uncomfortable with the lack of conversation in schools, homes, and medical offices about the side effects and risks of the long-term use of some medications. I'd heard stories about schools that labeled children, especially boys, as having behavioral problems and pressured their parents to put them on ADD medication. The drugs seemed like an easy alternative to deeper and more time-consuming approaches. I wondered how many children across the country were taking drugs when they really just needed a change in their diet.

Even family members who knew very little about Matthew's condition were waving the medication flag at us as if it were a miracle cure. They swore by the results they claimed to have seen in other children with ADD —but not autism.

Dr. Childress' thoughts on medication and Sonya's were in harmony. Later, I would accept the fact that my position would have to be surrendered for a time, but not before I had held out for another two years.

Chapter Eight

MADE USEFUL

Give, and it will be given to you...

- Luke 6:38
(NIV)

FROM AS FAR back as the time of Matthew's birth, we managed our pain and angst by turning off the world and concentrating on our own needs. By 2009, our personal lives had been turned upside down. We were short on answers for Matthew, and our emotional and physical fatigue persisted — Sonya expressed it in her way, and I in mine. However, the radical rise in the number of American families struggling with similar burdens was forcing us to consider that what was happening within the walls of our home went far beyond a personal affair. Sonya and I felt God prompting us to consider how we might be a part of His response to the profound increase in autism rates among children.

We did not know what this revelation meant or what it would lead to. It had been years since Sonya or I spearheaded a charge to help teenagers and the disadvantaged in any organized way, and our energy tanks were often so low we could not picture ourselves leading a crusade against autism. With our regimented lifestyle of appointments, sleeplessness, and anxiety, we were barely hanging on in many ways. If we were going to do anything for anybody, it was not going to be like our former lay-ministry days, when our personal desires took a back seat as we ran full steam ahead to the aid of others. Instead, in a gradual and tempered manner, we began to take deliberate notice of what was going on around us and became open to whatever God might bring about.

One of the first opportunities for us to get involved was an annual fundraiser held in Atlanta by a national organization involved in autism advocacy and research. The fundraiser involved a five to seven mile walk in which participants formed teams and raised money by gathering pledges. On the April morning of the event there was heavy rainfall, and the forecast was no more promising for the afternoon, so Sonya drove to the midtown location of the walk with her cousin while I stayed behind at home with Matthew. In spite of the weather, thousands of people attended the event and it was a great success in terms of raising funds and bringing attention to the crisis affecting so many families.

By the time the event ended that afternoon, the sun broke through the clouds, and it was a beautiful day. Sonya returned home rejuvenated. She was moved by the gathering of so many people around the central issue affecting our life—some there as professionals involved in treatment or therapy, but most just parents like us who were just as bewildered and stunned by autism as we were. Sonya's enthusiasm was inspiring, and I decided I would definitely attend the next year's event.

SPEAKING

IN CONNECTION WITH a local social media Web site's autism awareness efforts, the public relations department at The New Center for Autism Progress asked me if I would write an article for a blog, and I agreed. The subject was the effectiveness of dietary interventions on autistic children. I enjoyed writing the article, and I was satisfied with how it was presented on the Web site among a larger collection of video interviews and other articles on related topics.

In six or seven paragraphs, I candidly shared our experiences with Matthew's dietary interventions up to that time, and what, if any, changes we saw in him as a result. At some point after the article was posted on the site, I reread it and realized it really did have value for others who might be considering dietary interventions. My aptitude to write meaningfully on the subject was not necessarily the result of a literary ability; rather it was because of the life we had been living. It was a small-scale step, and I don't exactly know how many people read the article, but it was one of the first practical signs our hardship could produce something of meaning for others.

Later that year, the same public relations department asked if we would be willing to participate in a phone interview about our experiences with Matthew, which would allow them to get to know us and possibly mine our responses for remarks useful for autism awareness materials. We agreed.

The phone meeting was set up for late afternoon in the middle of the week. When the interviewer called, we had technical difficulties with our speaker phone, which prevented Sonya and me from being on the phone at the same time, so Sonya ended up doing the interview alone. She was asked various questions about our lives and the impact having a child with autism had on us personally. The interviewer also wanted to know how we believed The New Center for Autism Progress helped us. Sonya closed out the conversation by agreeing to participate in future efforts to gain support for the fight against autism.

We did not hear back from them for many weeks, but one evening, as we were preparing for dinner, they unexpectedly called. I answered the phone thinking it might have been a telemarketer or survey company.

"Hello."

"Hello, may I speak to Mr. or Mrs. Powell?" The woman on the other end of the line was friendly and cordial.

"This is Mr. Powell."

"Hi Mr. Powell, this is Tina McNair at The New Center for Autism Progress."

"Oh hi Tina." Tina's name had been given to Sonya as someone who might possibly contact us. "How are you?"

"I'm good. I was calling to see if you and your wife would be willing to participate in a radio interview in support of an upcoming autism event."

"Sure."

"Great, the date will be March 31st, at seven in the morning. That's a Wednesday. Still interested?"

"Sure," I said, while instinctively trying to think through how we would get Jaida and Matthew to school on time and then make it to wherever this interview was going to be. I figured it would be a small, local radio station near Matthew's school.

"Good," she replied, "It will be with WHZUR 88.31, and we can talk beforehand about what the interview will be like."

WHZUR 88.31 was the highest-rated African-American R&B radio show in Atlanta, with a listenership of millions. In addition to broadcasting the show by radio in the morning, it was televised in the evening. The host of the show was considered a celebrity in Atlanta, and she regularly interviewed well-known stars in the studio. I could not believe we were being asked to participate in something of that magnitude.

"Ok," I replied, trying to not sound nervous.

"Do you listen to the show?" Tina sounded as if she was wondering why I was not jumping up and down at the fact we were going to be on the program.

"Oh yeah," I said calmly. "We listen to it when we're driving Matthew to early intervention."

"Good," she said. "Don't worry about what you'll say. We

can help you with that. As the date approaches, I will contact you again with more details and we can talk things through." I was smiling really big on the other end of the phone as I thought about how unlikely it was for us to be asked to be on a major radio and television station.

"Thanks for doing this." Tina said.

"No problem," I replied. "Talk to you soon."

"OK. Goodbye." As she hung up the phone, I realized I was not completely clear on what we would be talking about. Nevertheless, I was blown away we had been asked to participate.

I knew Sonya would be super excited because she listened to the show much more than I did.

"Who was that?" she asked, before I began to speak.

"It was Tina from the public relations department at The New Center."

"Oh, what did she want?"

"They want us to be on WHZUR 88.31." Sonya paused and raised her eyebrows.

"What do you mean?" she asked, as if she had heard me wrong.

"They want us to be on The Juliet Morning Show." I knew she would be shocked.

"Are you serious?"

"Yes. In support of the upcoming autism awareness events, they want to have parents of autistic children on. I don't understand all of the details, but she said she would call us back as we got closer to the date." I paused. "Can you believe that?" I asked.

"Yeah, it's amazing." Neither of us could imagine little ole us receiving such a request.

Very early the morning of our interview, we dropped Jaida off at daycare. Matthew went to our close friends Vern and

Annette's home, and Annette would take him to school later that morning while we continued the interview.

At the studio, we were met by Salina, the morning show's producer. She was a tall, energetic, fashionable woman who was responsible for making the morning show run smoothly. She introduced herself and seated us in a waiting room down the hall.

She also introduced herself to a man sitting on one of the other couches who were reviewing notes inside a manila folder. He was a child psychiatrist, he explained, who saw young children with developmental or behavioral challenges. He was also there to be on the show.

By that point, we were starting to get butterflies, and we still did not know what to expect in terms of the direction of the discussion. The producer told us the topic of the show was "Autism in the African-American Community," which was different from what Tina at The New Center for Autism Progress had told us, but that did not affect our willingness to participate. However, our confidence was a little shaken when Salina told us the doctor who was to answer callers' questions had not yet arrived. I was terrified we might be put on the spot with questions we could not answer.

Salina appeared to be used to working through adversity. With a sense of urgency, and just short of losing her cool, she pulled out her cell phone. Her first call provided some information but fell short of contacting the missing doctor. It became obvious she was beginning to feel a little more pressure. With a hint of worry and a little less confidence in her voice, she said, "We need to have a doctor on the show," and, continuing to think out loud with a solution-oriented and determined attitude, she stated, "We already announced a doctor would be on."

"I am a doctor," said the man sitting on the couch near us.

"Oh," said Salina. "I thought you said you were a psychologist?"

"No," he replied. "I'm a psychiatrist. I'm an M.D."
"So you can respond to our listeners' medical questions?"
"Yes, I'm qualified to do that."
"Great! Then let's go in the studio and get started."

Salina led us into the room where Juliet Morris was, and she seated us in front of microphones. The on-air discussion went well, and we could hardly believe we were sitting in the same Atlanta studio that big-name celebrities passed through all the time. We were not star struck, but we were very aware the subject of autism was important enough to be addressed before millions of people.

The first questions were fielded by Dr. Coleman and focused on providing a general overview of autism, but also touched on complicated questions, such as why African-American children were typically diagnosed later than children in the general population. Then Sonya talked about our experiences with Matthew and shared what we thought was important for parents to do to try to get help. We emphasized becoming part of a special-needs community, whether it was a local support group, knowledgeable friends and family, or an empathetic church or large advocacy organization.

Originally we were scheduled to be on the air for about thirty minutes, but due to the overwhelming number of incoming calls, the show was extended to almost two hours. The station's phone lines lit up as tons of people tried to call in to talk about what they were personally going through. We again got the chance to see firsthand, as a result of our struggles with Matthew, that God had given us something to offer to others.

SPEAKING UP (ON VACCINATIONS)

EVEN THOUGH IT was eight-thirty in the evening, the last light of the sun had not completely faded. We had eaten dinner together as a family and Matthew was in bed, though not asleep. Jaida was awake and crawling within inches of Sonya and me with no particular interest other than to be as close to her parents as possible, with our undivided attention. Unfortunately, our eyes were glued to the television set.

The news anchor was interviewing a doctor about the cause of autism spectrum disorders and what progress was being made to find treatments. We were eager to hear how the doctor would respond—especially to the first part of the question.

We were also excited to see any public discussion of autism, because it meant that somebody knew we existed and cared enough to talk about it. We also hoped we might hear something new and helpful. Unfortunately, our cloud-nine anticipation of new insights quickly dissipated with the doctor's scripted answers, which seemed like fancy ways of saying "I don't know."

It was rare for us to go a day without wondering (and researching) not only what caused Matthew's autism, but also why it was on the rise nationally and globally. The latest statistics showed one in every 150 children in the United States was diagnosed with an autism spectrum disorder, and the rate was climbing. In New Jersey, where Matthew was born, the numbers were the highest in the country: one out of every ninety-four boys was on the spectrum.

We did not believe childhood vaccinations were the lone culprit, but we also did not believe there were no developmental health risks involved with them. Sonya and I were aware of the reports claiming there was no scientific evidence tying autism to vaccines, but the same entities producing them were unable to provide any solid reason for the prevalence of autism.

We would not be shamed into changing our position out of a fear of appearing to be unintelligent parents who were overcome by emotion and unable to understand scientific method. We were overcome by much more than emotion - our son had a lifelong disorder. We were open to having our minds changed, but any answer short of disclosing the reason for the tidal wave of new cases remained suspect and subject to scrutiny.

Since we knew there was a risk of exposure to disease if Jaida and Matthew were not immunized as they entered school and society, we did not choose to skip vaccinations altogether, but we pursued routes we found more assuring. We decided to decline a number of Matthew's booster shots beyond what he had already received. As a safeguard for Jaida, we presented her pediatrician with an alternate shot schedule. Because the number of vaccines given to children at one time had significantly increased over the years, we decided to spread them back out to allow her immune system to be stronger during each round of shots. We also decided to not allow Jaida to get a shot unless she was completely free of illnesses at the time.

At one of Jaida's visits, Sonya let Jaida's pediatrician know we wanted to use an alternative schedule for Jaida's immunization shots.

"I have a question," said my wife to Dr. Jones.

"Sure, what is it?" she replied with a smile.

"We have a son who is three years older than Jaida, and he has autism. We are concerned about vaccinations and we want Jaida to receive all of her shots by the time she is old enough to go to school, but we would like to use an alternate schedule. Would you be able to accommodate us with that?"

Dr. Jones had an immediate response that sounded partly like a question and partly like a statement.

"Well, you do know there is no connection between vaccines and autism."

"We have a son with autism and my husband and I are not comfortable with Jaida receiving shots in a way that has any type of questions or controversy around it. Can you accommodate us?"

"If you put it in writing I can take a look at it and then get back to you," she said calmly.

"Thank you."

Later on, Sonya and I sat down at our dining room table and drafted a letter to Jaida's doctor. By now, doctors were accustomed to parents showing up and asking questions, if not outright refusing immunizations for their children. A few years earlier everyone just got on board. We personally delivered the letter during Jaida's next well visit. It read as follows, and included a photocopy of an alternative vaccination schedule:

Dear Dr. Jones,

As discussed at Jaida's last visit, enclosed please find a copy of the alternate vaccination schedule we would like to follow (schedule starts on bottom page of the enclosure). Upon your review, can you please call us to let us know if the Pediatrics Office can accommodate this schedule? Additional information we have referred to is included.

Thank you in advance.

Sincerely,

Paul and Sonya Powell

Dr. Jones agreed to follow the schedule we provided. We appreciated her willingness, especially because we knew she did not agree with this protocol. Through a number of similar experiences, Sonya and I learned we must advocate for our children.

OTHERS

ONE OF THE most significant ways Sonya and I were able to be a part of the solution to autism in our society was to simply pass on to other parents and caregivers the hope and help we were receiving. One afternoon while I was at our local library, I was working intently in a small study room that had an old-fashioned chalkboard on one wall and a large glass window pane on another, through which I could see the main library floor. A woman who appeared to be in her early to mid-fifties approached a table outside the window and sat down. She had with her a stack of papers tucked under her arms. She laid them on the table in front of her.

I was certain the woman looked familiar, although I could not figure out where I may have known her from. As I turned my attention back to my work, the feeling I knew this person grew, but I still could not figure out where I could have met her. When I could not take it anymore, I stepped out of the study room and went to greet her, hoping she might recognize me. As I approached the table where she was seated, the woman looked up, smiled right away, and said "Hi, you're Matthew's dad." It turned out she was one of Matthew's teachers from a summer intervention program he had participated in a couple of years earlier. Her name was Sheila.

Sheila was glad to see me but was more somber than I recalled. She and I sat and talked for a little while and she told me she was now caring for her ten year old nephew who had a disability. Her face showed the strain of the restless nights and adverse days that accompanied caring for a disabled child. She talked about the distress she now experienced and about how she had sought out a parent support group to get help. She was noticeably different from the person my wife and I previously sat with in a meeting room discussing Matthew.

Shelia and I talked for about fifteen or twenty minutes, and she admitted to me that now that she was caring for a special-needs child of her own, she realized she never truly understood what the parents of the children in the intervention program really went through. I empathized with her concerning the pressure she was under, and I tried to inspire her. When we finished speaking, Shelia was genuinely refreshed – and so was I.

Unfortunately Shelia's situation, like ours, was becoming increasingly common. There is barely a store, school or public event I can go to without meeting someone who knows someone who is affected by autism or a similar impairment. This means there are countless people in need of someone who can relate to their unique troubles and serve as an agent of healing.

There is considerable work to be done on behalf of children, adults and families suffering through disabilities, and it can appear to be an agonizing feat to determine where to begin the task. God began to put in the hearts of my wife and me a dream of helping thousands of people, but as He brought it to fruition in His own time and in His own way, we were happy to share the hope and love we were receiving from Him with one Sheila at a time.

Chapter Nine

GOD USES PEOPLE

Angels are merely spirits sent to serve people...
   - Hebrews 1:14
   (CEV)

THERE WAS NO denying the ancient African proverb, "It takes a village to raise a child," was true for our family. Whether it came from relatives, friends, or strangers, taking care of Matthew and Jaida meant enlisting the help of other people—each with their own unique experiences, gifts, temperaments, and perspectives. At times, help was defined as moral support when nothing seemed to be going right; at other times, it was calling one of our parents for their input on a particular situation. Sometimes, we just needed a babysitter, Sunday dinner with cousins, or a play date so our children could make friends.

More often than not, we deliberately sought out professionals and parents from whom we gathered invaluable understanding about how to do our best for Matthew. In some instances, however, with little to no effort and in the most unlikely situations, we unexpectedly met people who opened up our minds about how to care for Matthew and ourselves.

A DEPARTMENT STORE PROPHET

IT WAS NOT an altogether rare occurrence for our whole family to shop in a mall department store, but neither was it common. We were not casual shoppers, and, usually it was a pending special event or holiday that motivated us to buy clothes. In this case, it was because we were going to visit Sonya's family for the Fourth of July and she needed something suitable to wear during the exceptionally warm season. Matthew, Jaida, and I were just tagging along.

Sonya picked out a few articles of clothing to try on, a couple of summer blouses and a long matching skirt, and headed off to the dressing room. The kids and I remained outside in the waiting area, which was small, but comfortable, with a long leather bench against a wall and television monitors flanking both sides, which were airing animated-children's programs. I was holding Jaida in my arms and Matthew was lying on his side and rolling around on the bench taking in the programs. Periodically, I caught his arm as he attempted to make a dash for the clothing racks ten feet away under which he found it so much fun to crawl, feeling the fabric brushing across the top of his head.

While we were waiting, an African-American man with graying hair and a very friendly disposition came and stood near us as his wife disappeared through the same dressing room doors Sonya went through. We smiled politely at each other and began to speak:

"Hey, how are you," I said.

"Pretty good," he replied with a warm smile. "He looks like he's having a good time," referring to Matthew who was giggling and rubbing his hands on the smooth leather surface of the bench seat.

"He *is*. I'm the one doing all the work." I said jokingly, as I stepped two feet to the right again to prevent Matthew from running off. "He'll take off and never look back if I let him."

"He wants to explore and see the world," the man said warmheartedly, "He's just learning. Kids are amazing. I can tell he's smart." He leaned in Matthew's direction to get to his attention. "You're havin' a good time aren't you buddy?" Matthew's eyes were fixed on the television monitor, and he did not acknowledge the man's words or even turn his head in the man's direction. I waited a few seconds to see if Matthew would respond, but he did not. Untroubled by Matthew's lack of response, the man pleasantly remarked "See? He's just takin' it all in."

I was used to people producing a puzzled look on their face at this point, as if to ask why Matthew did not respond to them, but this gentleman did not. "He has autism." I said, feeling responsible to make this proclamation when someone had gone out on a limb to speak to my child. I wondered if I would have to go on to explain what autism was.

The man did not seem affected by my words in one way or the other. Keeping his smile and friendly composure, he just put his pointer finger up to his lips and referring to Matthew said, "Shhh, don't tell him, he doesn't know it," as if to say don't label or limit him.

The man's wife came out of the dressing room at the same time as Sonya, and the couple said good-bye and walked off, leaving me in awe of the graceful and inspiring thoughts this stranger left for me to consider.

A FELLOW TRAVELER

I CASUALLY WALKED through Newark Liberty International Airport in New Jersey on a Friday afternoon after finishing a week of work at my company's office. I was returning to my wife and children in Atlanta, and experience taught me to get to the airport early to avoid the inevitable Friday evening flight delays.

After checking in at the terminal kiosk and going through the security checkpoints, I had a little time on my hands, so I stopped into one of the terminal convenience shops to buy a bottle of water and some trail mix. The store was set up in such a way that, as soon as your feet left the corridor and stepped into the twenty-square-foot space crammed with newspapers, candy and gum, you were confronted with wall shelves lined with magazine covers and strategically placed waist-high racks holding bestsellers on various subjects. Side stepping the shelves and avoiding close calls with other shoppers, I happened upon some book covers that raised my curiosity about their contents.

Snagged into the retail trap, my eyes rested on a book about autism. It was the story of a young man's personal experience, and, given where my life with Matthew was at the time, it was nearly impossible not to pick it up. I rested the five-by-eight-inch paperback in the palm of my hand and read the review and summary on the back cover before deciding to buy it. As I stood in the line to the cashier's counter, a woman standing nearby went out of her way to start a conversation with me. She was Caucasian with short brown hair and a petite stature. It was winter time, and she was wearing an expensive-looking fur coat. Initially, I was not sure what to make of her.

"I've read that," she said, looking at the book and not at my eyes.

"Was it good?" I asked uneasily.

"It was helpful. I've read books by a few autistic adult writers."

"Oh, really?" I said, beginning to feel uneasy because I did not know where the conversation was heading with this complete stranger.

"Do you have a boy or a girl?" she asked in an empathetic

tone that implied she knew something about my life and could relate to it.

Her last words evoked my understanding that she was the mother of an autistic child and wanted to connect. I was relieved to be a bit clearer about why she was speaking to me, and I replied with a warm smile, "I have a boy. He's four years old."

"I have a boy also. He is severe. We have tried many different treatments over the past two years."

"Have you seen changes?" I asked, wanting some insight into what we could expect to see with Matthew, and possibly some hope.

"Unfortunately not."

"We took my son to see a doctor in Connecticut."

"Dr. Samuels?" she asked. I was surprised she knew exactly who it was, and I was reminded there were not many physicians practicing in the way Dr. Samuels practiced.

"Yes," I said, noticing another woman in line was listening to our conversation.

"Is your son verbal?" I asked.

"Not at all," she responded, "And we really have tried all sorts of treatments. My husband does very well, so we have been able to try a lot of therapies. We live in Chicago, and we have taken him to one of the leading autism doctors there." I sensed she was in a fight to keep her spirits up.

"It's really hard. These are our children. We just can't give up." I said, trying to offer encouragement.

"No we can't," she replied.

"Good luck. I've heard it gets better."

"Same to you, and I hope so. Nice to meet you."

I paid for the book and left to take a seat in my flight's terminal. It was refreshing to unexpectedly come across someone who allowed me to unearth my pain while moving through the chaos of a world in which packing your burdens in a bag as if they did not exist was the thing to do. I felt a little sad and wished I had stayed to talk with her longer.

Once on the plane, I tried to picture in my mind what the woman's son looked like and what her life must be like with a child who was more severe than Matthew. I thought about the look on Matthew's face when I tickled him and how he laughed until he could barely breathe and then came back for more. I considered again what it must be like for the many parents of children with life-threatening illnesses, and I realized as a result of a brief, random conversation, I was able to slow down and be thankful for my son. I was not sure I had fully learned the lesson of gratitude for what I have, but my memory had been jogged.

SWIMMING LESSONS

"THIS MIGHT BE something worth looking into," my wife said to me as she held out a copy of a flyer that came home from school in Matthew's backpack that afternoon. It provided details about swim lessons for special-needs children at a local community swimming facility. I hadn't given much thought to the idea of Matthew swimming. I guess the fear we experienced from his attempts to dive into the duck pond escaped my memory. "Oh, that sounds good," I replied unenthusiastically and trying to not get an attitude at the thought of another appointment to drive to. I tried to hide my selfishness by adding, "Why don't you call for more information?" with a quiet, exasperated sigh.

Sonya was unmoved by my subtle opposition and heeded my suggestion, not my sentiment. Within a week, we were driving Matthew to swim lessons at our county's new aquatics center. The instructional leaflet we received requested parents remain in sight of their child throughout the lesson and they arrive at least ten minutes early. I was driving fast because we were close to being late. We had never been to the aquatics center before and we did not know what to expect in terms of parking, signing in, or other administrative matters.

As we sped down one of the many two-lane back roads in our county, heading to the swim facility, we wondered how the lesson would go. We were nervous and tried to prepare ourselves for whatever might happen. Was the instructor someone who we could communicate with easily? Was the instructor someone whom we could trust and whom we wanted to interact with our son? What if we liked the instructor, but Matthew did not? We hoped he would enjoy the water, but, because of our fair share of past disappointments, we knew it was at least possible it might not go well.

We drove through an unlocked, modern, black iron gate and pulled into a horseshoe driveway in front of a large building with three sets of glass double doors. While Sonya parked the car and helped Jaida out of her car seat, I hurried Matthew inside. Upon entering, we signed in at the desk, which was between the doors we had just entered and another set of glass doors beyond which we could see two pools below a naturally lit ceiling that looked like it was at least forty-feet high.

The larger pool was divided into lanes, and it was adequately sized for the high school swim meets as well as full-gear, scuba-diving lessons. The other pool was about half the larger pool's depth and seemed to be more for recreational swimming. We asked for Bill and Lindy, the instructors who were listed on the flyer. The desk attendant directed us to the smaller pool. Although Matthew was humming and fidgety, he was excited by the sight of the water on the other side of the glass.

By now, Sonya was in the building, and we went into the pool area as a family. Our nostrils were met with the warm, humid smell of chlorine. Bill and Lindy were in the smaller pool, and they greeted us from the water. Lindy was warm and energetic. She had a big smile and a southern accent with a somewhat raspy voice. Bill was less animated than his wife, but he was no less pleasant. He smiled when he introduced himself and seemed genuinely concerned about making us feel comfortable. I undressed Matthew down to his swimming trunks and helped him over to Bill in the water.

Matthew looked very uncomfortable and afraid as soon as his feet hit the water, and he started crying to get out. Our first reaction was to take him out, but we were determined to give him a chance to get used to the water. Bill was gentle and careful as he led him around the water by his hands, without letting Matthew's face fall below the surface of the water. This went on for about five minutes. All the while, Matthew's petition to get out of the water did not subside. He continued crying and saying "All done, all done please! All done, all done please!" Bill remained calm, trying to reassure Matthew that everything would be OK as he continued to give him a chance to get used to the idea of being in the water.

At some point, while Matthew was still pleading to get out, Lindy, who was working with another small child in the same pool, turned and commented that Matthew probably had enough for his first day. Bill brought him to the side of the pool where I was standing, and, as I wrapped a towel around him and took him to the locker room to change, I wondered if Matthew would get used to being in the water, and if we would follow through with additional swim lessons.

Following through with swimming was the best thing we could have done for Matthew. His first day of lessons was not an indication of what his overall aquatics experience would be. Matthew grew to love swimming and his instructors. Sometimes, he swam with Bill, but mostly it was with Lindy. And, if she were free after his regular thirty-minute lesson ended, she swam with him a little longer.

Lindy was caring toward Matthew, and she never failed to encourage him. Previously, Sonya and I experienced service providers who lacked the sensitivity to see the little boy with feelings beneath the autistic behavior. Lindy could not have been further from that type of person, and Matthew built his own relationship with her.

Throughout the next months, Matthew's smile seemed to exceed the sides of his face during his lessons. He loved to repeatedly jump into the water and create big splashes. "Readyyyyy, sehhhht, goooo," was the alarm sounded by his high-pitched voice, indicating he was about to leap from the edge of the pool into the air. In reality, he was only jumping two feet away from the edge, but in his mind, it was as if he were diving off a cliff. With one raised and outstretched arm and his knees pulled up near his stomach, Matthew produced a splash twice the size of his body before vanishing below the water's surface. He reappeared within seconds, swam about three feet back to the side of the pool, climbed out, and repeated the sequence again.

Lindy was methodical and patient with Matthew's development, and, by watching her I learned how to be more patient with him and leave room for his natural growth. She coached high school swimming for mainstream students, and she and Bill were veterans in the area of working with special-needs children. To me, it was evident she knew where his progress in the water was heading, but it was hard for me to see it. I just knew Matthew enjoyed the experience and it was good exercise for him.

Although Matthew loved to swim, and it was fun to watch him in the water, his lessons became somewhat regimented and, typically, not full of surprises. An exception to this occurred one Saturday morning when something reminded me, with the help and concern of forces seen and unseen, the sky was the limit for Matthew.

Normally, his lessons were on Sunday afternoons. After rushing out of church following the last song and benediction, I sped down Route 20 to make it home in just enough time to pick up Matthew and take him to his lesson. However, this week, due to scheduling changes, Lindy and I agreed to switch his lesson to ten o'clock Saturday morning.

Coming out of the locker room, Matthew and I carefully planted our feet on the pool steps and held on to the stainless steel rail descending into the shallow end of the pool. My grip on Matthew's wrist was loose as the comfortably warm water rose first above our ankles, then knees and thighs, before we stretched out and waded among the other children and adults who were enjoying the four-foot-deep water. On this particular Saturday, I brought my swim trunks so after Matthew's lesson was over, he could continue to play in the water. More often than not, I just handed him off to Lindy at the edge of the pool and hung around reading a book or observing. After another minute or so, Lindy came over and Matthew went off with her, holding on to her shoulders because he could not yet swim on his own.

When his lesson ended thirty minutes later, Lindy's next student had not shown up, so she continued with Matthew. He was joyful holding on to Lindy and performing his diving routine. Matthew was barely aware of the other people in the water because he was having such a good time. As they played, Lindy led him under the water every few minutes so he could get used to holding his breath.

As time passed, Lindy incrementally allowed Matthew to have more independence in the water. She was relaxed, not pushing him or even trying to work him up to the next level, instead, she supported him as he initiated what he wanted to do. At some point, as I watched, she began to support his body weight by placing her hand under the center of his back as he lay in the water looking up. This went on for a few minutes until suddenly Matthew innately tilted his head back, looked up at the skylights, and he began to float on his back—free of Lindy's hand. He smiled as he took in the feeling of floating, and he was as comfortable as a fish in the water. It was hard to comprehend what was going on in his mind, but he was happy. I looked at Lindy in amazement because, fifteen minutes earlier, Matthew could not let go of her arm without sinking.

With his head back and toes up, he continued to lie on the rippling, blue water for a minute or so before putting his feet down to gather himself, and then, float again. After another few minutes of this exercise, and without any prior indication, he unexpectedly turned onto his stomach, took a breath, went under the water, and swam away from us as if he had been swimming for years. I was overwhelmed. There was nothing Lindy had been trying to teach Matthew that looked even remotely similar to what he had just done. It was just *in* him, and he had reached a point where he was comfortable enough to act on it.

Lindy had probably seen this many times before. I had not. Suddenly, I understood what she was envisioning during all those months working with Matthew and what she saw as his future capability. I realized all the times she had said in passing he would be a good swimmer, she was not just being nice—she meant it. By the age of six his swimming form was still a little unorthodox, but Matthew swam well enough that I did not have to worry about him diving into the duck pond anymore, and he had the promise of continued growth.

A good example to me and Sonya was Lindy's character and spirit. Lindy and Bill cared deeply about people with special needs and disabilities, to the point they lived a life devoted to serving the disabled in their professional and personal lives. They knew the history of special-needs services in our community and county schools, and they were a wealth of information, wisdom, and encouragement. They became our friends.

Through Lindy, Matthew learned to swim, and, in the process, on that particular Saturday, I awoke to the fact that he is always learning and progressing. God designed him to do just that. It was evident to me we should not lower our expectations for Matthew's development; instead, we should raise our level of faith, endurance, and patience to gradually see his growth.

ANGELS COME IN ALL SIZES

ON THE WORN grass and dirt-patched field, which was adjacent to the parking lot of the rural church we were visiting in McIntosh, Alabama, from a distance I observed a profound social and psychological event. "Ready, set, go!" shouted five-year-old Kyle excitedly as he lined up his body next to Matthew's and took off running without looking back. The son of my wife's first cousin, Kyle was a vibrant and energetic little boy who could not get enough of playing outdoors. With all of his might, he sprinted to keep Matthew from winning his rightly deserved "Olympic Gold Medal." As Kyle reached his make-believe finish line, he celebrated his victory briefly before peering back to see how close Matthew had come to beating him.

Back at the starting line, Matthew stood quietly looking at the magnificent sight of ants trailing one another on the ground. He was not doing any of his usual stimming or pacing, but he was so mesmerized by the tiny, brown creatures he barely heard what Kyle was saying:

"Ok, Matthew," said Kyle, undeterred by Matthew's disregard for the track meet rules, "Let's race again. We start when I say go. 'Ready, set, go!'" Kyle took off again with the same athletic determination and love for the game he exhibited the first time around. After celebrating his second win with a big smile, he ran back to the spot where Matthew was still ant watching, and kicked off the third heat by explaining the rules to Matthew again.

I was heartened by what I saw. Matthew's lack of response

did not prevent Kyle from enjoying his company, which generally went against the rules of engagement for young adults and grown-ups. Given the opportunity, I hoped Kyle and Matthew would become friends as well as being cousins. We were always concerned about what kind of a social life Matthew was going to have as he grew up, and we believed it was our role to help him maintain friendships, as well as help his friends understand him. However, watching Kyle's play helped me to relax some and remember God would put the right peers, in the right place, and at the right time, for Matthew.

HORSEBACK RIDING WITH RHONDA

WE READ ABOUT hippo therapy for special-needs and disabled children in different magazines and special-needs resource books. As a result, we researched venues in the Atlanta metropolitan area providing this service. They all claimed speech, social skills, anxiety, and other deficiencies, which accompanied developmental issues, could be addressed, though not necessarily cured, through guided horseback riding with a trained therapy specialist. Some riding organizations stated the developmental benefits from riding came from practicing physical balance and bonding with the horse.

Personally, I did not have the slightest idea how all this could happen on the back of a horse. I was not what most people referred to as an "animal lover," and I had no knowledge of horses. I had been on a horse only three times in my life, and two of those times were for-hire services with horses so tame or old even I knew it was nothing like what the real experience of riding should be. However, there were enough testimonials from people we had spoken with and on the Web to get us to take hippo therapy seriously. Even more important to us than those claims, was that Matthew adored animals.

In keeping with our plans to follow Matthew's interests, Sonya and I talked a lot about finding a place for him to be able to ride horses, even though our budget was limited. We thought we would just have to find a place we considered affordable and then raise the money. We considered garage sales, bake sales, or even letting family know they could contribute money to support Matthew's riding instead of buying him the usual birthday or Christmas gifts.

After kicking ideas around for a couple of months, while other life matters continued to take precedence, Sonya decided to call a well-known riding stable not far from Matthew's school. It was located in a prestigious area, and I was sure it would cost a lot of money, but it turned out to be reasonable. Sonya scheduled a riding session with someone at the stables named Rhonda. Rhonda was a certified therapeutic riding instructor and had trained with a physical therapist for about a year. She was well prepared to work with Matthew. Even though Matthew would not be able to tell us verbally, we knew that, for him, to get on the back of a horse would be like a dream come true.

A TIME TO RIDE

EVEN THOUGH HALF of our family could have taken the opportunity to get a little extra sleep, we decided we would all go to Matthew's first riding lesson. It was dark outside in October at 6:30 AM and, on top of the normal morning wait for daylight, the sun was hidden behind a hazy drizzle and thick fog following the previous night's rain. We explained to Matthew he would be going to ride a horse, but he was not yet able to comprehend the concept, apart from actually doing it. He did not know where we were going but he loved the morning and was more than willing to get out of bed when I woke him up. It was one of the few times I would actually get up before he did.

We made yet another drive northward from our home and headed east on Route 20. With all the daily trips back and forth, our little sports utility vehicle felt like our second home, and every inch of the highway scenery was embedded in our minds like a photograph. It was hard to not feel exasperated and borderline bored when we merged onto the interstate. The only thing we could count on to add some variation to the drive was the weather, a good radio talk show, and, occasionally, taking an exit we had not used before. On that morning, the last of these three, along with the anticipation of seeing Matthew's reaction to horseback riding, made our commute somewhat interesting.

We got off the highway nearly forty miles away from our home and followed our directions through a number of twisting, two-lane local roads before reaching the horse park. Both Matthew and Jaida were alert and taking in the scenery trying to figure out where we were. We parked in a paved lot, which was uphill from the stables, and we walked down to meet Rhonda. Sonya and I wondered how she would respond to Matthew. We assumed she would be experienced with special-needs children since she knew in advance Matthew had autism, but we had no way of knowing whether she would be mechanical and businesslike or make a real connection with him. We had encountered both before, and if she were cold in any way, we knew it would nullify the magical experience we were hoping Matthew would have.

Rhonda did not disappoint us. She met us with an authentic smile containing no hint of a sales pitch. She was an average-height, thin woman in her late thirties with long, blonde hair tucked under a baseball cap. Her Midwestern accent and obvious passion for horses matched her blue jeans, pine-green windbreaker jacket and well-worn, dusty, brown riding boots. As she said hello to Matthew, she was unmoved by his focus on the acre of moist soil beneath his feet instead of her voice. Overall, she seemed just nervous enough to meet us to indicate she was sincere. Her assistant, Shelly, was just as amiable.

"Hi Matthew," Rhonda said, again making eye contact with Matthew, "Would you like to ride Cobalt?"

"Yes," he replied in his typical, high-pitched voice that sounded a little robotic. He definitely now had some sense that he was there to ride, and he looked around, spellbound by the many horses sniffing the morning air through the barn windows or grazing in the outdoor stables. In proportion to his growing excitement, Matthew mumbled comforting words to himself as Rhonda fitted him with a riding helmet and took his hand to help him onto the small horse named Cobalt.

Our hearts lit up as Matthew's face drew up a smile he attempted to hold back, but could not. We were persuaded the driving and the stretch to pay for the lessons would be well worth it. We agreed Matthew would ride every Friday morning at eight o'clock. It was apparent to us Rhonda was passionate about horse riding, special-needs children, and the connection between the two. She had two school-aged children of her own, and yet, she was willing to get up and come work with Matthew on frigid mornings just before her weekend started.

Rhonda interacted with him wonderfully, and she encouraged us regarding how well autistic children interacted with animals and how well the horses responded to them. She said they comforted each other. "Matthew had a natural awareness for how the animal feels," she stated several times. It was difficult for me to understand what she meant, until one morning, weeks into his lessons; Matthew backed away from Cobalt and refused to mount him. Later that morning, the stable manager told us Cobalt was not feeling well and required medical attention. "You see," said Rhonda, "Matthew knew it, even when we had no idea. They have a connection."

Matthew's riding lessons included him being led around

an oval-shaped, covered area where Rhonda and Shelly taught him to say basic riding commands; such as, "Walk on, Cobalt," and "Trot, Cobalt." In addition, they practiced alphabet identification with large wooden letters posted at various intervals on the fence enclosing the riding area. Rhonda also worked on Matthew's balance by having him pick up rings hung on posts in the riding area and placing them on other posts. His favorite part of the lesson occurred when they left the covered area and headed out to a wooded trail. When they returned to ride in the covered area for a little while, Matthew would say, "Trail please. Trail please." I asked Rhonda what was so great about the trail, and she said there was something about the peacefulness of the outdoors the kids just seemed to love.

From week to week, Matthew's attention and ability to follow directions ranged from clear to inwardly focused and fidgety, with no apparent cause for one or the other. Sonya and I guessed it was connected to the amount of sleep he got on Thursday nights, but, as usual, we were unable to pin it down. What was interesting, however, was his behavior reports from school on Friday were good, and his teachers noted he seemed calmer than usual when he rode that morning. Rhonda said it was because of the horseback riding, and we tended to believe her.

When the heart of the winter arrived, we bundled up Matthew in a wool hat, heavy coat, and gloves, and we continued to make the early morning appointments until it was obviously too chilly for him. The temperature kept decreasing week by week until he was no longer able to hold the reigns and follow Rhonda's instructions. Instead of paying attention to her voice, Matthew kept placing his fingers in his mouth, even with his gloves on, for stimulation and warmth. Eventually, the December weather became too cold to continue to ride, and we had to break until it became warmer. This was disappointing, but it was also a blessing in disguise because we were starting to have difficulty paying for the lessons, and we needed time to get more money together.

Rhonda's commitment to working with Matthew reminded me of our own devotion to Matthew. She was cheerful and immovable through adversity, whether it was us canceling a lesson due to illness or getting to the stable late due to the morning traffic. One clear illustration of her sincerity happened months later when the weather started to warm up, but our financial situation had not improved. We had been unable to raise money for additional riding lessons, and we simply told Rhonda we would contact her when we were ready to bring him back out to the stables. It pained us to not be able to give Matthew something he enjoyed so much, which was so good for him, but we accepted that was how it had to be until things got back on track. One evening, weeks later, I was checking our family email and came across a message from Rhonda:

Hi Paul and Sonya,

I hope all is well and I really miss having Matthew at the barn. If you are interested, I would like to privately fund Matthew's riding at [the horse park]. I know timing was difficult with school and all, but think about it and let me know if 8 a.m. would work for you again on Fridays. Then, when summer rolls around, we can get flexible with some better hours if you want. Or, if you just want to wait until summer, which is fine too—this offer has no expiration date (It has been bitter cold out there these past mornings, so I can see waiting until this cold snap passes.

Just let me know your thoughts on this or if you have already found another barn.

Happy New Year and stay warm!!

Rhonda

We replied:

Wow! We are amazed and grateful. 8:00 AM on Fridays would work after the weather lets up a little.

[We] will give you a call.

Thank You!!!

Soon after Rhonda made this offer, Matthew was back riding at the stables. There were no words to express our gratitude. Matthew was as happy as ever to see Cobalt again and to get back out on the trail. It was a complete joy for me to watch him up on the horse, smiling again, in the early morning sun. It was humbling for me to accept Rhonda's help, but Matthew riding again outweighed my pride, and gave me a sense of relief similar to the feeling of having fixed something that had been broken.

THE RIGHT TEACHERS

IN MATTHEW'S THIRD year at The New Center for Autism Progress, Sonya enrolled in a master's degree program at a local university. Her major was education, and she took a course with a nationally recognized expert in special education practices within K-12 schools. Several times during the semester, this professor stated his many years of research and observation of special education programs at numerous schools led him to believe the success of a developmentally delayed child's educational progress was not dependent on the geographical region, institution, or school system. According to him, it was not even due to the amount of money spent on each child, rather the individual teacher who worked with the child.

I do not know whether my wife's professor perceived the key ingredient to effective teaching as genuine concern for the student, or as a deep knowledge of instructional practices, but Matthew's teachers at The New Center were living illustrations of his point. Most of Matthew's teachers were either behavioral or developmental specialists, or were studying in a related field on a graduate level. Because they worked at The New Center, not only did they have a high level of knowledge and competence about behavioral interventions, but they were also continually exposed to real-life situations.

On a practical level for Sonya and me, Matthew enjoyed school and liked attending on a daily basis. He could not communicate this, except to say, "I want school please," but, on many evenings as he rolled around in his bed trying to wind down, he would repeatedly ask for one of his teachers by name and say "I want tomorrow. School please." To us, this meant he had fun in his learning environment, and he felt secure there.

Sonya and I thought The New Center did many things well with the early intervention program. We had the sense they were very on top of things and always looking for ways to make the early intervention program better. However, more impressive than their organization and forethought was their ability to identify the right kind of people to work with children who ranged in degree and type of developmental delays. The New Center recruited people who seemed to have a gift for working with special-needs children and who possessed the essential ingredient required to effectively help them - genuine empathy and concern.

If there were ever anything the teachers at Matthew's

school lacked in knowledge, it was made up for in heart and character. It is a known fact people in their field can burn out within as little as five years or less due to the demanding nature of the work. Yet in all the days we trekked from our southwest Atlanta suburb to the north side of the city, we could not think of one day when any one of Matthew's teachers did not greet us with a smile or ask us how we were doing. I am sure there was some obligation to professional duty, but there was never even a single day in which they exhibited an attitude about our mishaps.

Parent guidelines had been set to manage the arrival and departure of children in an orderly fashion, but the teachers never put us on the spot if we stepped outside them. On the contrary, they always seemed to understand what we had to go through to get Matthew back and forth to school each day. There were a few days each week, when one family or another arrived at the school just late enough to find an empty playground, which minutes earlier, had been full of backpack-toting children being kissed goodbye by their parents. Their decision to not humiliate us while taking the extra step to sign our child in at the front desk because we were late was an act of grace. This meant a great deal to harried, stressed-out parents like us, who, on most mornings, usually faced some type of household or highway adversity.

We could only imagine what it would be like if we had to regularly, or even occasionally, engage in guilty explanations about being late or forgetting something at home. The teachers who worked with our son exhibited patience in our presence, which we knew carried over into the classroom. They were genuine. As a result, our days were not filled with lingering questions about how Matthew was perceived or treated during the day. Instead, we were confident that while he was out of our sight getting the help we could not provide for him at home, he was being nurtured by people who more than anything else, cared about him.

SPEECH THERAPY

Matthew was a little distracted this week. I tried both a morning and an afternoon session to see the difference. He was really grabbing for things during the session, which he has not done before. Other than that, he had great eye contact and worked hard as always! We sequenced two to three cards using proper pronouns (he has been using "your" and "my" instead of "him and her"). For example: "She is washing my apple," when it should be "she is washing her apple." Try to work on "her," "him" and "their." We also worked on "where" questions, "when" questions—with pictures, and understanding negatives in a sentence. I would show him three objects or pictures "Which is not a fruit, food, drink shape?" etc. Teach him to point to it and say, "This is not a shape...it's a food." He did really well with answering functional "why" questions.

THESE WERE THE written comments from Matthew's speech therapist, Chrissy, regarding a session she had with him earlier during the day. Chrissy could be best described as someone of exceptional skill and extraordinary passion, and I had met few people in few professions who, similar to her, were doing in life what I would consider exactly what they were supposed to be doing. She was overflowing with energy and had a God-given ability to help special-needs children learn to communicate and interact with others.

Chrissy was a sincere Christian with a genuine faith in God, and she did not separate her profession from the work He had given her to do. She was not *just* providing speech services to children; rather I got the sense she was the type of person who woke up in the middle of the night with new ideas about how to help people. Chrissy and her husband were raising two children in whose hearts they were instilling compassion toward others. As a family, they participated in charitable events, mission trips, entertaining special-needs children, and they had even started a non-profit organization to raise funds for underprivileged children.

She was a real-life superhero for special-needs children and a source of insight for Sonya and me on creative ways to motivate Matthew. She was especially focused on helping him to develop social awareness, and she was pivotal in helping us identify healthy and fun ways Jaida could participate in his development through natural play such as taking turns and imitation. She kept our eyes and minds open to new ideas, which was critical because we periodically reached points when we felt stumped.

As a parent, you know when someone does or does not care for your child. Call it a sixth sense, hunch, or intuition. You just know, and it makes all the difference in the world when you are deciding whom you want near them. Chrissy was someone we wanted in our life and close to our son. She could no more promise us results with Matthew than we could guarantee ourselves, but her competence, refreshing optimism, and extremely hard work provided a much-needed boost to our faith about the possibilities for Matthew's future during some really wearisome days and weeks. We believed she was sent.

EVEN MATTHEW

WE PACKED MATTHEW'S bag and said goodbye to Jaida and Sonya. I fastened Matthew snugly into his car seat and pulled the top of the strap to ensure it was secure. I was in high-spirits about what had become our Saturday morning father-son routine. We would drive to the county aquatics center for Matthew's weekly swim lesson with Lindy. Following the lesson, Matthew and I pulled up to a nearby drive-through restaurant window for the only fast food he would eat – fries. From there I deliberately turned our drive home into a slow-moving excursion. I took delight in the two of us just being together without the pressure of having to be somewhere.

Matthew had a good time in the water with Lindy that morning. As they wrapped up, I met them at the poolside and draped a beach towel over Matthew's back. He briefly resisted leaving the fun behind, but then, as if his thoughts were suddenly swept to some other place, he surrendered and moved on. I prompted him to say thank you to Lindy and we headed toward the locker room to change.

At the time, Matthew's echolalia was prevalent and he continually repeated the last word spoken to him while simultaneously asking how to spell the same word. He was doing this as we were transitioning away from the pool.

"Did you have fun," I asked him, prompting him to speak and keeping him focused on where we were going.

"Have fun," he replied, "how spell have fun?"

I obliged him, "Fun is spelled f-u-n."

"F-u-n," he repeated.

As we entered the blue and white ceramic tiled locker room, there was a noticeable drop in temperature. The chilly air was initially stinging, but it did not seem to bother Matthew. However if I, being fully clothed, could feel the difference in temperature, I was certain Matthew was cold. I pulled his towel a little tighter around his back and moved quickly to help him change with as little exposure to the cold air as possible.

"Are you warm," I asked Matthew.

"Warm. How spell warm," he said.

"Warm is spelled w-a-r-m." I realized that this could go on for a while, and at that moment, I did not want it to.

The locker room changing stalls contained lemon yellow, concrete benches, and though I am sure the concrete facilitated sanitary conditions, the benches were frigid. It made me all the more eager to help Matthew change rapidly; which was hard to do because rather than cooperating to change out of his swimsuit, he was distracted by every inch of the locker room environment. This included, but was not limited to, his reflection in the mirror, the voices of other people, the squeaking of his soft, rubber swim shoes against the wet floor, and the sound of running water in the showers. He would have normally been overwhelmed by so much activity, but at that moment, he seemed intrigued and excited by it.

The ceramic wall surfaces caused sounds in the room to reverberate. A single voice would immediately bounce from wall to wall as if in an echo chamber. Matthew inadvertently discovered the echo while accidentally vocalizing something like a yelp. As soon as he did it, he was enthralled by the immediate amplification of his voice. He looked at me with a big smile celebrating his discovery and proceeding to do it again, and again, and again, and again.

I was self-conscious about the noise Matthew was making, and the fact that he was doing it repeatedly. I could not tell exactly, but it seemed he was getting progressively louder and more excited each time he let out what now sounded like a loud cry of some kind of bird. I began to wonder what some older boys not too far from us were thinking, and I became even more uncomfortable. I was purposely calm and discrete but firmly told Matthew to stop yelling. No sooner had I told him to stop, he did it again.

At his opposite reaction to my instruction, I became aggravated. I lowered my eyebrows, pointed my finger, and sternly said to him, "I mean it. Stop yelling." Matthew's unhesitant reply to my gestures was, "How spell *angry?*" Ashamed, I stopped in my tracks. Matthew had called me out on my anger, and I felt like a thief who had been caught in the act. His interpretation of, and response to, my expression was unusual for his comprehension level at the time. He had not been taught the word *angry*, and for him to appropriately apply the term in context, was remarkable. I believe the message to me was to "cool it"; and Matthew was the messenger.

Chapter Ten

FINDING PEACE

So neither the one who plants nor the one who waters is anything, but only God, who makes things grow.

- 1 Corinthians 3:7
(NIV)

EVERY TIME I saw a flash of progress in Matthew's development (such as hearing him properly use a short phrase he had learned in the right context, or watching him write a new word), my tendency was to want to will him to greater growth. Rather than savoring the victories, I took them as signs that with more effort, Matthew could reach even greater heights, and I pushed harder for the next developmental win. Likewise, when Matthew experienced a day, a week, or a month in which he could not break away from stimming or stay seated for two minutes, I felt deflated and wondered what I was doing wrong.

In time, God brought me to a place where He allowed me to see that making peace with autism was essential if I was ever going to leave this heartbreaking cycle behind. Additionally He began to soften my heart to accept that doing so was not what I had believed in my heart for so long—which was working less was tantamount to abandoning Matthew. Instead, it would be casting off my self-reliant attitude about getting him well and replacing it with true faith and dependence on God. It was a sober admission on my part on who I was, and who I was not, to Matthew—his earthly father, not his Heavenly Father. There were things that simply were not in my power to do for him. Finding peace on a daily basis meant learning to be OK with that.

ACKNOWLEDGING MATTHEW

WE WERE IN the middle of our usual weekday early morning rush, one of the most stressful times of the day. The task at hand was to help Matthew put on his shoes. I was watching the clock and becoming uptight about being late. "Let's go, Matthew," I said. He did not seem to hear me as he stared at his hands, wiggling his fingers in front of his eyes in a manner similar to someone making shadow puppets. He was also quietly rambling to himself. "Let's go, Matthew," I repeated impatiently pointing at his black leather sneakers sitting on the floor two inches away from his feet. Matthew seemed oblivious to what I was saying and that his shoes needed to be put on. "Come on, we have to go." I was one step away from yelling, and I was clearly making Sonya uncomfortable. Jaida was eating a bowl of cereal seated at the table nearby. She paused and stared in our direction to see what I would do next.

"This is one of those times," said the voice in my head, "Remain calm, rational, and patient; there are bigger things at stake than just getting on a pair of shoes and making it to school on time." I thought, "I hate being late. Why can't he just move it? We've done this a thousand times, and we do it every day. I'm not his servant. He needs to put his own shoes on."

"Come on, Matthew." I blurted out again. My words were exaggerated and my frustration was no longer hidden. In response, Matthew wrapped his fingers around the lenses of his glasses to hide his face and began to cry. He heard me loud and clear, but the message he received was not about putting on his shoes or getting in the car on time. I had hurt his feelings. I knew I had crossed the line, and I immediately felt like a jerk. "Why did I let myself go like that," I thought regretfully. My guilt was as heavy as a mountain as I tried to apologize and console him.

Matthew appeared to be ignoring my instructions, but of course, he was not. He was just a little boy fighting the difficulties of autism as best he could through the many physical and mental distractions that plagued him. This was a reality I still needed to control in my mind, even though the only thing apparent to me at times was what was visible on the surface.

As we embarked on the morning's drive, I could not shake off my guilt. Matthew was sensitive, and he did not move on quickly either. He would not just hop in the car and play with an electronic game or toy and forget about what had just transpired. The damage was done, and he would sit in his seat, sad and hurt for a while. My outburst would most likely stay in his mind until we arrived at school and he saw other children on the playground. I wished I could just pay a fine to make the dreadful feeling inside me go away, but that's not how things worked.

Fifty-five minutes later and barely on time, we pulled into the school's parking lot. As we exited the car, Matthew wrapped his fingers around the lenses of his glasses to hide his eyes, this time not out of discouragement, but out of excitement. He loved school. This was not something he could verbally articulate, but it was obvious. He chattered softly to himself in an attempt to manage his enthusiasm about entering the playground near his door. I felt thankful because he was no longer thinking about the incident with me. I escorted him through the gate into the playground, hugged him, and said goodbye.

As I walked back to my car, I was still upset with myself

for losing my temper with Matthew. I knew he would be OK this time, but this was not the first time, and he would not be all right if it became a pattern. If I were going to prevent history repeating itself, I needed to be profoundly honest with myself as I grappled to get to the root of my anger. I wrestled with my thoughts, which were, on one hand, reflective and, on the other hand, defensively refusing to admit there was something about me that called for serious examination and change.

I made a left onto the residential street leading out from the back entrance of the school. It had several speed bumps that forced me to drive slowly. It would be another ten minutes before I reached Interstate 85. I had all the time in the world to think. I turned my thoughts over in my head repeatedly urging myself not to evade the pain that was bound to come from looking at how I mistreated Matthew and not to pretend I was better than I really was. Inside me, I knew I had been blowing it with my son.

"What was really behind my frustration?" I asked myself, agonizing over the question. As I thought as candidly and as objectively as I could, it gradually became clear that, over the course of time, I had lost sight of the wonderful little boy God had given me. Instead, I was viewing him through the lenses of autism and its related hardships. It hurt me to admit it, but I was more focused on fixing Matthew than on Matthew himself. My interaction with him was teetering primarily on something project-oriented and secondly on a father to son connection, as if he was inherently not good enough. I was slow to look past his autistic characteristics and simply enjoy our relationship. I had become the father who pushed his child too hard, thinking it was for their own good, without assessing what his child thought or felt. I did not accept Matthew for who he was. And, as a result, I was often not much fun for him to be with.

"Of course you accept him," objected a voice in my mind in mid thought, "He's your son. He's the only son you have."

"No, you really have not accepted him," said a second voice, pleading with me to remain honest.

"Then why would you do all that you do for him?"

"Doing for him and accepting him are two different things."

"But, but…"

"How would you feel about him if he never grew one step more in his development than where he is today?" I paused using the question to examine my motives. I visualized Matthew as an adult living in our home, with limited verbal communication, and having little social life and no occupation. I tried to imagine how I would feel about him in that situation. I tried to figure out if I could just let him be, without trying to force him to go in a direction I deemed best for him.

"It's your job to deem what is best for him," said the defendant in my head.

"Yes, it is," said his nemesis, "but you should act from a standpoint of what is best for *him*, not you."

At this thought, I made an attempt to imagine what it would be like to ease up on my insistence that Matthew progress beyond certain autistic symptoms. I felt a little release of pressure, and it occurred to me I might be inflicting a lot of pressure, not only on myself, but also on Matthew, Jaida, and Sonya. Again, I felt torn apart inside. This type of inflexibility was one of my character flaws, and had reared its ugly head before.

"Admit your mistakes and go forward," said my rational inner voice, "Matthew is a person, just like you. He has likes and dislikes. Just because he can't verbalize his feelings doesn't mean he doesn't have them. You have probably hurt him many times." My guilt tripled. A third voice of reason told me to not make it about me, that my guilt was not productive, so don't wallow in it, just change quickly and move on. This registered with me, and I resolved to strive to be different.

Autism was hard to live with because it exposed *my* imperfections. Often, regardless of what was going on in my life, I wanted to appear to the world as if everything were going well. In some sense, I tried to live in a normal house, drive a normal car, and pursue a normal profession to comfortably fit into my surroundings. Like much of our society, I wanted to look good, and I was afraid of what others would think about me if I did not. I liked to view myself as being stronger than that, but my actions and thoughts often said otherwise. Unless it was something widely recognized and esteemed by others, I was not looking to stand out in the crowd.

Having a child with autism did not allow Sonya and me that luxury. We could not fade into the background of our neighborhood or community when we met someone and Matthew did something socially inappropriate. When he randomly yelled in public or mimicked the voice of a cartoon character or video game, our mask was removed.

I had a good thirty minutes before I arrived home. My introspection was profound, and I knew that it needed to be. The things I was seeing in myself were hard to swallow because they implied, whether or not Matthew ever talked in full sentences or expressed how he was feeling, I had to learn to interact with him as the person he was, not the person I wanted him to be. I was not sure I knew how to do that. It brought to the forefront of my consciousness a feeling of deep uncertainty about his future. I also realized my head had been in the clouds for a while, and the truths that were being unearthed were not going to quickly sail away.

Recognizing my mistakes was the first step, but getting where I needed to be would take more than that. Matthew was growing. He had his own will, opinions, and desires. He *really* was his own person, interacting with the world in his own way. Regardless of what I or anyone else thought about it, this was his God-given right. I had to own up to the truth, that as I tried too hard to assist him in his development, I intruded on Matthew's individuality.

Old habits would not die easily - there were ups and downs. I prayed for a sincere and lasting change of heart. I presumed my transition was similar to what all parents experienced at one time or another as their children grew and they had to learn to respect them for whom they were, not for whom they wanted them to be. I also knew that my request to change was the type that God would honor. Sonya and I had no intention of lowering the bar for Matthew's health or his educational needs, but, as I discussed with her what I was seeing about myself, we began to work together to build a relationship with Matthew that encompassed more than just acting as caregivers.

IDENTIFYING STRENGTHS

IT WAS OBVIOUS that Matthew was bright. He learned to read words quickly, and he easily translated that to reading in sentences. I was not always sure how much he comprehended, but I think it was proportionate to his knowledge of concepts. Reading sentences such as "Matthew is riding the horse in the barn," was no problem, but something conceptual, might be a little harder for him; such as, "It is cold in the house." Matthew did not particularly like sitting down to read for too long, but he seemed to really enjoy the feeling of trying to figure out a new string of words and getting it right.

Matthew had progressed far beyond the days of watching balls roll past him. Now, he kicked soccer balls back and forth with others and verbally expressed anticipation of receiving the ball back once he booted it away. Matthew also progressed well beyond just hitting plastic softballs off stationary tees. He still loved to do that, but, even more, he enjoyed the thrill of connecting with a ball I pitched to him and watching it sail off through the air. His coordination was good, and he handled it well when he missed a pitch. I enjoyed this about him.

Matthew was a sponge, learning new things extremely fast when he was motivated. During one vacation at Sonya's cousin Rhonda's house in Birmingham he exhibited this trait with a video game of all things. Rhonda and her husband Mike had three children ages three through ten. In the bottom floor of their split-level home was an enormous wide-screen television on which Mike watched sports, and on which the children played classic video games, such as Pac-Man. One afternoon Matthew was attentively observing the other children as they skillfully navigated the animation character along a video maze of dots, and dodged pursuing digital creatures.

After observing for a while, Mike directed his children to let Matthew have a turn. Matthew fumbled with the joystick clumsily, and his character on the screen was repeatedly eliminated in record time. Mike attempted to assist him with the control and I tried to cheer Matthew on yelling, "Run, run, the monster's going to eat you." over and over. Initially, it seemed pretty unlikely Matthew would figure out how to properly play the game. I could see by Mike's facial expression that he was beginning to feel pretty sorry for Matthew. However, having witnessed Matthew in similar situations many times before, I explained to Mike that, ever since Matthew was a toddler, he had an aptitude for electronic toys of any kind. I told him if we just left him alone with it long enough, he would figure it out.

Matthew played with the game off and on throughout the remainder of the day, and did just as I thought. The following morning, as we prepared for the next leg of our trip, I asked Mike if he had gotten the chance to see Matthew play Pac-Man since he had first tried it. Mike replied with some amazement that he definitely saw Matthew's ability to hammer away at something until he got it. He was impressed because, after a noticeably slow start, Matthew moved on to independently maneuver his way around the game and obtain high scores.

Matthew also had an uncanny ability to concentrate when

he was involved in any kind of artistic activity. Whether he was at home or at school, it was unlikely that an onlooker would be able to distinguish him from a typically developing child. Clearly, this was one of his strengths. There was something about positioning himself in front of a large piece of paper and a container of water, tempera paint, and a brush that brought him to a place of serenity and clarity. For whatever the reason, those conditions allowed him to defy the distractions of his sensory issues and attend to details in a manner that normally was not possible. The extent to which creating visual art soothed and directed his thoughts was beyond our comprehension, but we knew he liked it, and we applauded this achievement.

RESPECTING MATTHEW

Today Matthew sat and went through his box of sixty-four crayons and collected all the ones that are some shade of blue. I wonder if he found the blue ones pleasing, or if he just liked having similar colors together.

- My Journal Entry

EIGHT FANS SUSPENDED from the high vaulted ceiling of our church's main worship room rotated in chorus. They spun tirelessly yet barely put a dent in the warm air generated by the congregation's singing, clapping, and swaying to the gospel music flowing from the band on the stage. Matthew tolerated the sound and crowd for as long as he could before placing his hands over his ears and saying, "Outside please. Outside please." Stepping over a number of people seated between us and the aisle, we exited the sanctuary with as little disruption as possible. However knocking a bible or two to the floor and bumping into a few knees was unavoidable.

Once outside we saw other adults, children, and teenagers who for various reasons were also not participating in the service. We had thirty minutes to kill while Sonya and Jaida stayed inside through the end of the sermon. The church was on a side street in an urban neighborhood, and was surrounded by blocks of row houses, apartment buildings, and commercial outlets. Both sides of the streets were lined with parked cars.

There was about fifteen feet of fading green lawn between the church entrance and the street. Without delay Matthew knelt down and pressed his fingertips into the grass. He was determined to find out if it felt as good as it looked to him. His fingertips sunk into the soil and he appeared to be happy with it. After about a five minute span a little boy about Matthew's age strolled over and initiated in playing with him; but Matthew did not respond. Instead he abandoned pressing his fingers in the grass and moved on to look for bugs.

After repeated attempts to get Matthew to acknowledge him, the boy approached me with a request for intercession. "I'm trying to get him to talk to me," he said, "but he won't." I felt bad for the boy because he genuinely seemed disappointed that every time he came near, Matthew ran off to some other spot. "Why don't you try to talk to him again?" I suggested, not knowing what else to say and realizing there was no way to explain autism to the boy. As I looked on, he went over to Matthew and tried to engage him again with no success. Then, he came back to me and said, "I was trying to play with a bird one day, and every time I tried to go near it, it flew away in the sky." Pointing to Matthew, he said, "He's just like that."

I did not disagree with the little boy's analogy. I found it hard myself to understand Matthew at times. It was important to take time to consider what the world might be like from his point of view. I imagined it to be remarkably different than my own.

At age six, Matthew's sensory issues were less apparent than they had previously been, but they were a primary influence on his feelings and interpretation of situations.

In some cases, Matthew had a heightened, positive experience—like the sensation of feeling water on his skin when he swam or took baths. It was evident he was having a positive encounter with the world by his lack of anxiety or distraction from other sights and sounds around him. At other times, his experience was not so pleasant. Noise was his most obvious annoyance, but light could also be an issue. When Matthew slept at night, he put his head under his blankets to block out any light; he was very comfortable in a jet-black room. It was almost as if it gave him a chance to take a break from mentally organizing the information he saw, heard, smelled, and touched, and just get some rest.

Even with what we could tell through daily observance, Sonya and I assumed we did not get half of what life was like through our son's eyes. We only knew it was important to facilitate situations that brought out his best behaviors, and limit environments that impeded his ability to function and learn. While this was not *always* possible, it was *often* possible, and we consistently approached new situations with a mindset of enabling Matthew to try new things before deciding which was which. In this way, we began to follow his lead in knowing him better and letting him provide us with clues about his world. It helped us with learning to respect him.

ACCEPTING CHANGED DREAMS

IN THE SPRING of 2009, we attended a weekend long conference for families with autistic children. Our accommodations were at an attractive luxury resort that had private recreational grounds. Whether it was the dining room or a bench in the lobby, ornate and high-quality design surrounded us. It did not feel gaudy; rather, it was warm and inviting. Various family oriented activities were scheduled over the course of the weekend. Some were for the entire family; others included just the children or just their parents. To my surprise one of the parent activities that I found to be the most memorable of the three days we were there was a group discussion among five married couples.

The forum was held in a naturally well lighted, round meeting room that was as elaborately decorated as every other area of the resort. As we entered the room, it was noticeably quiet; even though we were the last husband and wife team to come in. Chairs were placed neatly around a table on the end of the room opposite the entrance. On the periphery of the table was an exquisite banquet table with pastry, fruit, and vegetables. I thought to myself that the resort hosts had gone to great lengths to make us feel comfortable. Oddly enough, the only thing on the table that had been disturbed was a crystal pitcher of water and a few glasses.

We had not been told what we were going to be doing, and there was a man in the room that I did not recognize from our earlier welcoming activities. He was African-American and appeared to be in his late thirties. He was dressed in a business casual manner, wearing a dark blue suit with an indigo shirt but no tie. The man was clean cut, well-shaven, and wore contemporary, black-rimmed glasses. He had an unintimidating demeanor that I felt combined with the refreshments and quietness of the room screamed out *group therapy session*. It was pretty clear that everyone felt a little nervous and was wondering where things were headed. Sonya and I were no exception.

"My name is Jeff Hilson," the man said serenely without warning. "I am a licensed psychologist on staff at Therapeutic Southern Family Services or TSFS, who sponsored this weekend of rest for you and your children." Jeff's demeanor was humble and his pace of speaking and tone of voice was supportive, as if to articulate every word in a way that ensured no one in the room was left feeling unclear about what he was expressing. I got the impression that he and whoever else organized this gathering had given a lot of thought to who we all were.

Jeff continued his introduction, "I specialize in family stress and relationship concerns. I have been with TSFS for three years, primarily as a resource to families such as yourselves who are managing one or more special needs children." He set the tone for what I was now calling a session, by explaining it was just a time to talk and all comments would be confidential. I felt skeptical. He added that participation was voluntary. We were free to stay or go, to let off steam or just listen in. After that, he simply stopped speaking and sat still with one of the least judgmental and most candid personas I had ever seen in my life.

The silence was so obvious for the first few minutes that it was uncomfortable. No one said anything. Jeff made no attempt to coax anyone to speak. Everyone seemed to be wondering what an appropriate first word would be, and waiting for someone else, when the sound of one woman's cracking voice gingerly replaced the quiet. Her eyes were fixed on the tabletop before her as she faintly began a monologue about the painfulness of her nine-year-old son's disability. After speaking less than ten seconds, she paused and leaned her body closer to her husband for support. As if out of nowhere, she lost her composure, and she began to sob terribly. I breathed deeply to try to hold myself together. To outsiders, the woman's actions might have seemed perplexing. However, as parents of special-needs children, we all knew why tears were barreling down her cheeks.

Within the span of another thirty seconds, everyone in the room was crying. It was the last straw for wells of restrained grief, previously only mentioned to a spouse, if at all. Parent after parent began to express what they were dealing with and how they felt about it. Some spoke about hurtful words spoken to them by insensitive people; others spoke of their difficulties in adjusting to the restrictions of a special-needs lifestyle, which they now had no choice but to live.

The more we talked, the more honest the exchanges became. It was a seriously touching atmosphere, which I found liberating from the routine grin-and-bear-it requirement. A lump swelled in my throat when Sonya began to speak and tell of her personal difficulties managing life with Matthew.

After Sonya finished speaking, I wanted to comment, but I was so overwhelmed that I could barely imagine expressing myself clearly. I was torn between wanting to say something that others would find meaningful and spilling out pent up anxiety. Of the countless thoughts crowding my mind, the one premise I found myself able to grab on to and verbalize was that, after years of dealing with autism, only recently had I begun to no longer feel as if something had gone terribly wrong when Matthew had been diagnosed. Instead, I now comprehended that, because God does not make mistakes, *my son, and the course that our family's life had taken, was not a mistake.* I did not know how my remark fit in with all that had been said throughout the discussion, but witnessing the exchange of empathy and strength among everyone in the room, despite their pain, convinced me even more that it was true.

I knew Matthew did not fit society's, or sometimes, even Sonya's and my notions of a person who accomplishes esteemed tasks in the world, but, in my heart, I knew Matthew was exceptional. Whether I ever came to understand all the details of it or not, Matthew really did have a distinct purpose in life that was from God. Sonya and I were here to help him fulfill it. We were responsible for influencing Matthew's growth en route to the things he *could* do, while supporting him in things he could not do.

I had always dreamt of having a son who would become a man of character and integrity, someone who would be strong, tough, and ethical in his approach to dealing with matters of right and wrong. The artistic side of me pictured us one day sitting around talking about philosophical concepts such as why people behave the way they do or how to influence change in urban communities through film and other artistic expressions. I did not care whether he got a doctorate degree, but I imagined he would learn from me and his mother to do his best. I hoped he would be a man of faith who would love God and willingly help those less fortunate than himself.

I am not the type of person who hopes his children will be rich and famous or on television someday. That's not my nature. When I picture that sort of life I immediately think about all the unfavorable stories in the news about the lives of celebrities. Sonya is less of a "black and white" thinker than me. She is more capable of seeing the positive side of an acclaimed life because she believes the end result has everything to do with the individual personality. Sonya and I saw our children from different viewpoints, but we always agreed we wanted great things for them.

Matthew reminded us there were new dreams to be had, even in our own lives—dreams not centered on the rat race for money, acclamation, or even a prestigious profession; instead dreams predicated on the deeper things spoken of in the Bible such as a caring, contented, and unconditional relationship with our child for as long as we lived.

GROWING IN COMPASSION

OVER THE YEARS, whether or not I am at my best as a parent has been a strong indication of whether or not I am being a man of strong character. With the exception of my marriage, I can't think of any other area of my life that reveals and reflects who I am as much as my relationships with my children. And, in the many areas of my character that have been exposed as lacking, I have realized that changing me is not my work. It is a task much too hard for me to tackle alone. My job is to be alert to the reality that the work is required, and, as much as I can, appreciate the fact that God loves me enough to do it.

There seemed to be endless days when obstacles arose in our family life due to autism, and I found myself without the strength to overcome them. I needed to grow personally and spiritually, and adversity was progressively at work providing the opportunities through which I would have to learn. Facing family illnesses, financial troubles, and relationship challenges required me not only to mature in how I handled hard times, but also to view them in a different way. When I began to link the many changes we were going through with my ever-increasing ability to endure misfortune, I saw up close and personal how God had been using it to shape me.

Even though I continued to long for easier days, I neither sunk into despair nor tried to muscle my way through situations pretending they did not hurt. I was learning to draw on the battles we had previously encountered when approaching new ones, confident that things would work out for our benefit. The ability to look at Matthew's disability with a somewhat positive outlook was coming after more than six years. Formerly, I may have philosophically entertained the thought of that type of perspective, but I had neither the energy nor the will to hold on to it.

The area of my character in which I believe I experienced the most obvious change was compassion, especially for those who either are disabled, or live with or care for a disabled person. I had a long way to go, but prior to having Matthew in our life, I barely noticed physically, emotionally, or psychologically disadvantaged persons. I could not remember having an opinion about them one way or the other. Consequently, I never had any inclination to lift a finger to help them.

Matthew took me beyond the bounds of just having a heart for physically and mentally challenged persons, but ignited my concern for people in any circumstances who were less fortunate than I. Helping others had been something I did as a participant in church outreach efforts, but a deep and personal desire to lighten someone else's pain was not who I was. My own daily longing for relief gave me the desire to relieve others from their suffering. The homeless person standing on the shoulder of the highway, whom I used to pass by, suppressing the inclination to empathize with them, now received my attention. My own need for help facilitated an understanding of the power of kindness. There had been so many days over the past six years when personally, all I needed was for someone to let me know that they cared.

GROWING IN PATIENCE

Be completely humble and gentle; be patient, bearing with one another in love.
- Ephesians 4:2 (NIV)

7 PM WAS the end of the evening for Matthew. My body was fatigued as a consequence of the day, and I was exasperated. After numerous, unsuccessful attempts to get Matthew to sit in his seat at the dinner table instead of launching out of it and flopping on the floor, I was fed up. With little success, Sonya and I commanded, warned, bribed and modeled the right behavior for him. Each of Matthew's inappropriate actions was imitated by Jaida, in her attempt to get the same kind of attention she perceived Matthew to be receiving from us.

In spite of the circumstances, we managed to finish dinner

and promptly give Matthew a bath before bed. I was confident the warm bath water would help calm him down, but it did not. Matthew was as tired from the day as Sonya and I were, and he was manifesting it in silliness. He splashed the water so turbulently that he drenched the bathroom floor, walls, and me.

It took everything I had to maintain my composure. I was tempted to waive the white flag of surrender and ask Sonya to come up to put Matthew to bed, but when he was so overstimulated, he could be rambunctious, and handling him physically was even harder for her than for me. Finally, when I could not take it anymore, I picked him up out of the bathtub, dried him with a towel, and tried to put on his pajamas as he repeatedly slumped to the floor, waving his hands in the air, and giggling uncontrollably.

There was no way to get Matthew to discontinue his tirade or to even understand the ordeal was amusing only to him. He was exhausted and he was showing it this way. In my head, I knew this, but I was still aggravated and getting more frustrated by the minute. By the time I got him dressed, I was worn out and did not perform our usual nighttime routine, which was putting lotion on his back, tucking him in, and kneeling beside his bed to pray with him. I just opened his door, motioned for him to get into his bed, and slammed the door once he did.

I felt a sense of physical and emotional relief the second I shut the door. The difference between trying to put him to bed and actually having him *in* bed was like night and day. In fact, I would have had a perfectly peaceful moment had I not had to deal with my guilty conscience resulting from getting angry and not taking the time to pray with him.

In dealing with Matthew and with God dealing with me through my conscience, I discovered that patience refused to be circumvented. Even though I was tempted to feel that the verse in the book of First Corinthians stating "love is not easily angered" was too high a standard for me to consistently live up to, I saw God's commitment to helping me grow. He would not let up or adjust His standard to my actions or thinking. He would forgive me every time I blew it with my son, but still make it crystal clear that I was just as wrong as the time before. I knew, as God cultivated in me a genuine dislike for my wrongful actions, He would help me get beyond them— in His own time and in His own way.

GROWING IN HUMILITY

"WHAT SHOULD WE put on this line," Sonya asked about the county form fixed before her on the dining room table.

"What line?" I asked.

"The one that asks for your occupation," she replied. I was in between jobs, and finding a position was proving to be a monstrous task, much more difficult than I imagined.

"Just put self-employed," I said, while really thinking "Put anything *except* that I'm unemployed." I could not even stand the sound of the word "unemployed," let alone to tell someone it referred to me. After all, I had a business and though it was not meeting our income needs, it was bringing in *some* income.

"You never know," Sonya commented, "Whoever reviews the form might know of something or need a project manager." I felt like I was admitting defeat if I noted on the form that I was not working. I had my pride and dignity to preserve.

Matthew's needs were directly responsible for humbling me in a number of ways. The options before me were often to either put down my defenses or to forego securing input or treatment for Matthew. Within a three-year period, we had repeatedly discussed private details of our health, finances, relationship, and personal history with numerous doctors, teachers, therapists, medical specialists, friends, identifying parents, and anyone else who appeared to have the ability or means to point us to the exit in the maze that had become our life. It was contrary to how I liked to manage information about our personal life. I was a very private person and selective about what I discussed and who I discussed it with.

In addition to conversations centered on getting help, we completed and signed enough forms, waivers, medical releases, and permission documents in doctor's offices, government agencies, schools, and private organizations that there should have been a profile on us in every corner of the state of Georgia. I had to abandon my pride so regularly and line up with a system of reasoning that was motivated by doing whatever Matthew needed us to do. Before long, I could not remember ever seriously caring one way or the other about whom I asked for help. The person or provider, whom I had previously wanted to keep at a distance, became as welcomed as someone bringing a cup of cold water in the middle of a desert. It was clear that some things were bigger and more important than me.

There were a lot of times when having a special-needs child induced the feeling of sitting in a rowboat on a colossal lake without oars. There were periods when we did not know what school Matthew should attend or when he should change schools. Some therapies and services were too expensive, while others were too far from our home. There were times when we could not tell if something we were doing helped Matthew's progress or hurt it. Not knowing the answers to so many questions about autism and various treatments Matthew required made the idea of not asking for help ridiculous, if not irresponsible.

GROWING IN HUMOR

WHEN OUR EYES opened in the morning, so did our sense of hearing. We lay still in our bed, listening sharply for the sound of humming that normally came from Matthew's room first thing every morning. Sonya and I were on the tail end of our night's rest. Matthew had slept for seven hours without waking up, and it was a pleasant surprise. It was like getting an unexpected Christmas gift in June. Typically, Matthew would wake up with all sorts of laughter and gibberish and then come downstairs to enter our bedroom. This morning, we could hear him, but he was a little more subdued than usual. We assumed it was the result of fatigue.

Sonya and I were both stalling to see who would be the first one to make a move to check on Matthew. We were already a few minutes behind on our morning schedule, but we cherished the last possible moment we could stay in bed. Sonya conceded. She stepped out of the bed and went to bring Matthew downstairs. I smiled inside and lay back on the mattress in the place where Sonya had been twenty seconds earlier. I could hear Sonya's feet as she dragged herself up the staircase toward Matthew's room, when I heard her voice, "Paul." she said excitedly. "Come here. Come here."

I leapt out of the bed and sprinted upstairs, having no idea what I would find and fearing the worst. I was sure Matthew had hurt himself. As I dashed up the stairs and turned left toward his room, I saw that Matthew had departed from his bedroom and was now in the playroom. As I reached the doorway, Sonya was holding Matthew by his wrist to keep him still. He was covered from head to toe in thick globs of Vaseline. I had left a twenty-six-ounce container of Vaseline on the entertainment center, and Matthew found it and enjoyed it to his heart's content. The container was empty.

For the next hour, we tried to wash the oily petroleum jelly off him with no luck. Matthew was as slippery as water on a plastic waterslide. He was covered so completely that we had to keep him home from school that day. All I could do was laugh.

For someone like me, who was prone to try to keep a handle on all situations at all times, the ability to step back and find the humor in a situation instead of overreacting to it, was divine. So often I had done just the opposite. God was softening my heart in that area too.

KNOWING GOD BETTER

"I WANT CHURCH please," said Matthew in his typical high-pitched intonation as his eyes opened and his head popped out from under his burgundy comforter. It was a gorgeous Sunday morning, and, for the past three weeks, he had been attending the children's ministry class with me. He enjoyed it so much that he began to wake up on Sundays asking to go to church.

"Ok, let's go," I replied with a big smile. I was encouraged that, after a long and agonizing period of trying to figure out how to worship as a family, things were finally falling into place. Even before getting married I watched some of the married men with their wives and children and imagined what it would be like to someday attend church with my own family. Autism had forced me to wonder if it would ever be possible, but now we were actually doing it.

I was like a kid myself, helping Matthew wash up that morning, and my enthusiasm was sustained as I packed his lunch and put a children's Bible in his backpack. It felt like the best thing in the world. Matthew was happy, and, on top of that, he liked the class and was accepted by the other children and the teachers. As we made the thirty-five minute drive to our church, I was convinced we were seeing the answer to our prayers, and I daydreamed about all the great things Matthew would learn in a fun and spiritually led environment.

We crossed Auburn Avenue and passed through the neighborhood in which Martin Luther King Jr. had grown up. Two or three blocks away and less than three minutes later, we parked outside of our church. Matthew's eyes lit up as he realized we had actually arrived. "I want church please! I want church please," he said in anticipation of singing and playing games inside. Energetically, we hopped out of the car, and, with Matthew held back only by my hand in his, we headed toward the door through which the children were signed into class.

Entering among other parents and children, we approached the check-in table and looked across the large, open area that accommodated multiple classes. I immediately felt a little uneasy when I realized that the couple who had taught the previous three weeks, and their assistant, Mary, who was familiar with special-needs children, were not there. Instead, there was a new husband and wife teaching team. I had planned to let Matthew go to class without me that morning, but under the circumstances, I decided to stay.

As it turned out, Matthew had a harder than usual time with the sounds and activities in the room that morning. He covered his ears and hummed, and, as was often the case, I tried to help him feel comfortable while having little idea what was bothering him. Unlike the teachers who had worked with him over the first few weeks, the new couple seemed uncomfortable. We made it through the two-hour class though, and when signing out, Matthew's behavior indicated that, in spite of his periodic discomfort, he was happy to have been there. I looked forward to bringing him back the following weekend, especially when I found out that Mary was going to continue to work with the new lead teachers; she just happened to be absent that particular Sunday.

The following weekend morning provided just as pleasant weather as the previous seven days, and we awoke to find Matthew's enthusiasm for this Sunday service was exactly the same. Sonya and I shared it as well. We carried out the same routine as the week before, and then we loaded ourselves into the car and drove to church. When we arrived, even Matthew's tug on my hand to hurry into the children's area was same. I was happy to oblige him.

As always, we stepped up to the sign-in table, and we were greeted warmly. Across the floor in the area where Matthew's class met, the same couple who taught the previous week was welcoming the children. Instinctively, I almost looked around the room to see if Mary were there as well; but she was not. I hoped maybe she was just running late, but I knew it was not likely. I wrote Matthew's name on the list for his class, got his name tag, and, with some hesitation about whether or not the morning would continue to go well, proceeded to the kindergarten table. As we came within reach of the group, one of the teachers nervously, but decidedly, put her hands up indicating I should not seat Matthew and said, "Uh, Mary's not here today."

I was shocked and caught off guard. For a second, I paused to try to process what had just happened. "OK," I said quietly, still trying to decide how I should respond. They had made a poorly considered gesture that I knew was not born from intentional harm, rather it stemmed from unawareness and a lack of knowledge on how to have handled the situation better. During the previous week, I had observed that the couple was on the verge of becoming overwhelmed—even with their basic class duties—so I could not say it was completely surprising. Their introduction to Matthew included his struggle with sensory issues, and that probably left them feeling pretty confused.

As I returned to the entrance table with my son to sign out, I tried to think of something we could do together that Matthew would enjoy. Clearly, he was disappointed, and explaining why we were leaving, after all of his anticipation to get there, was beyond me at that moment.

Courageously, we returned the following week and arrived to find Mary already there. Matthew attended class without me, and the report afterward was encouraging. I felt as if there were still hope. Unfortunately, the next week I pulled up to church with Matthew only to find out she was on vacation for the next three weeks. We got back in the car, and I tried to think of something to do to alleviate his disappointment and mine. Soon after returning from her vacation, Mary's volunteer teaching was over, and I decided it was best not to bring Matthew back at all.

The experience of taking Matthew to church was, at best, sporadic, and some weeks were heartrending. The uncertainty of not knowing whether or not a class would go well was not the problem; leading Matthew on with so much excitement only to have to get back in the car and leave on any given week was unbearable. Sonya and I also tried to bring Matthew, along with headphones and a video game, with us into the sanctuary, but his interest in doing that was short-lived. We spoke with the church leadership about a solution, not just for our family, but also potentially for other families as well. But, we had to be realistic: though it was a great church that met the needs of many people, it was not equipped to meet the needs of a moderately, autistic child.

After almost twenty years of membership in the same fellowship, this decision left us, looking for a new church home—one that could accommodate Matthew's type of disability. Drastically shifting the pattern of worship we knew forced us to stop and think about what God required from us. In the name of perseverance, I continued to go to service alone at times, hoping to keep my spirits up and my eyes on God.

We pressed forward by doing things such as listening to sermons online and visiting new churches. While most aspects of our Sundays were inspiring, our background of worshipping among a crowd of believers left us also feeling unsettled, as if something were wrong or unresolved. I wondered why God would make it so hard for us to go to church as a family. Sunday mornings had gone from a time of joy and praise to a peculiar and uncomfortable source of anxiety about whether or not we were doing all we could to please God. We were on a road that was indescribably different from anything we had ever imagined.

Our large community of spiritually minded friends was for the time being a shell of what it had been. We previously served and were involved in the lives of many people. Now we were barely serving anyone. We were at a crossroad, and, like an athlete who wanted to do what they knew they were capable of doing, but was prevented from doing so because they were plagued by injuries, I was brokenhearted, frustrated and disappointed.

The light bulb did not come on easily for me. I was pretty well rooted in the traditions I had been practicing, and, even when it did come on, I still needed time to accept it. Matthew was *one* of God's ways of redirecting, not just the activities of my life, but also my relationship with Him as well. I had a very nice, neat, and tidy understanding of who I knew God to be, I had an orderly routine of how I worshipped and served Him, and He changed it. He pulled the twenty-year-old rug out from under me and caused me to consider that the road on which I was traveling was not necessarily a bad or a wrong one, but it was not the one He wanted me to travel at that particular time in my life. The more I resisted this, the more I struggled with moving forward.

It took time and the work of God in my heart for me to trust Him enough to take any direction that He led me. Similar to the first days when we received Matthew's diagnosis of an autism spectrum disorder, I had to remind myself that with God, change is not the end, rather a new beginning.

Chapter Eleven

HERE COMES THE SON

WORK WAS DEMANDING throughout the course of the day. It was one of those high activity periods at my company when a great deal of assignments were due, and at what seemed like all the same time. I would be in the middle of scrambling to resolve one issue, and before I could complete it, I would receive an email or two on another urgent matter requiring resolution within hours. It felt impossible to keep up with the workload. By five thirty PM, I was frustrated and tense.

Sonya had experienced her own struggles throughout the day. Having to pick Jaida up from her morning pre-K program, take her to the library, run errands, and complete medical paper work for Matthew was taxing. It was intensified by the pressure to get it all done quickly enough to arrive home in time to receive Matthew off the school bus, and constructively occupy him until dinner time. There were plenty of opportunities to think about how much we needed a relaxing get-away. By the time evening came, Sonya was in a frame of mind similar to mine.

If the weather was pleasant, one of the ways in which we left the day behind and unwound, was by loading our family into the car and taking a leisurely drive without any particular destination. We turned on music, and Sonya and I might talk, or just ride in silence. Matthew and Jaida usually played in the back seat. Given enough time, we might stop to enjoy one of the local parks, or pickup dinner, whatever agreed with us most at the time. On that day, a drive was in order, and on the tail end of the ride we stopped in at a local grocery store to grab a few things. I ran inside while Sonya, Matthew, and Jaida waited in the car.

In ten minutes I returned to the car with the items we needed. I also picked up an apple for Matthew and a small pack of animal crackers for Jaida as a surprise. They happily received their respective treats and began to enjoy them. All was well, until Jaida decided to misbehave. In order to get her full attention, I momentarily confiscated her cookies. The result was a crying, saddened four year-old. As soon as Jaida's cry reached Matthew's ears, he paused from nibbling on his apple, looked me square in the eyes from his booster seat and said, "Give it back to her." In shock, I immediately obeyed his instruction, and then turned and faced forward in my seat.

Sonya and I just sat quietly for another minute or so, looking at each other and wondering if what we just saw and heard had really taken place. This was the first time we had ever seen Matthew empathize with another person. The boy we had known these seven years would step on a person's foot without even realizing he had touched them. In addition to empathizing, he used appropriate language to address Jaida's feelings, and communicated he understood what would make her feel better. If all that was not mind blowing enough, he addressed me while looking me directly in the eyes.

OVERCOMING

THE END OF one season had come in our family's life, and another was on its way. Though much had taken place, seven years had seemed to pass by quickly. Matthew was not a little baby anymore, and there were distinct differences in our life since the days he first received a diagnosis. Matthew had grown in a number of areas, including but not limited to his speech and his ability to learn. His short attention span hindered him at times, and Matthew's progress was up and down, but by intervention, prayer, and God's plan for his life, he was verbally expressing himself in four to seven word sentences, and continuing to progress.

By working with Matthew on spelling and reading at home, we noticed his aptitude for reading. I once had a conversation with the mother of a six year old who had autism, in which she told me her son taught himself to read. I did not fully understand what she meant at the time, but her words came back to me as I observed how quickly Matthew picked up words and word combinations. In one instance while speaking with one of his teachers at school, she told me they had been working on three letter words such as "rat," "mat," and "cat" when Matthew picked up a book with images of airplanes in it and said, "Airplane, A-i-r, p-l-a-n-e, Airplane," and smiled. We regularly began to receive feedback from Matthew's teachers and therapists, reinforcing what we felt we were seeing at home – Matthew had made significant progress and was capable of more.

As a result, Sonya and I made the decision to transition Matthew from the New Center and enroll him in public school. It was not an easy decision. We had grown accustomed to the love and care Matthew received at the New Center. However, we believed all signs pointed to a change, one that would include more academic input and interaction with typically developing peers. Our goal for Matthew at the New Center's early intervention program had been to help him overcome behaviors that were borderline severely autistic. We believed that goal had been met. He had attended the New Center for three years.

Our decision meant moving to a town in a county that had a fine reputation for educating and accommodating children with special needs. Through the large number of school-age children with disabilities entering public school, our current county school system made advancements in being able to meet the needs of this population since the time we had Matthew in early intervention at River Pond Middle School. Nevertheless, we had heard great things about one of the nearby counties and their inclusion programs and history of educating children like Matthew, so we relocated. Once settled in, we found out many other families moved to the area for the same reason. Even outside of school, it was a truly special-needs friendly county.

Once Matthew was settled into school, we were pleased with our decision. He liked his new environment and we did too. Having him attend a school of fifteen hundred students was a significant change. The New Center provided a small, family environment. However, in public school, Matthew was part of a homeroom class of seven other children who also had autism, and he was regularly given the opportunity to participate (with a paraprofessional) in classes such as art, music, and science in an inclusion environment.

The school enrolled a large number of children with disabilities, and the children who did not have disabilities were friendly toward them. On one occasion, Matthew's homeroom teacher told Sonya and me of a small group of second grade girls who, before the school bell rang every morning, would show up to Matthew's class to say good morning to him and the other kids in his class. His teacher had not asked these children to do this. On the contrary, she did not even know who these girls were. Knowing Matthew was in this type of setting boosted our confidence and security.

Matthew was maturing in other areas as well. I enjoyed his ability and willingness to pray. I initially wondered if he thought about his simple prayers, or just said them by rote, but later I saw confirmation, in a humorous way, that he knew what he was praying. Our earliest prayers together were at bedtime and our prayer went something like, "Dear God, thank you for loving us." I modeled for Matthew at first, but eventually he began to pray on his own. In time, we started praying before driving. We would buckle up in the car and before pulling off, stop and pray, "Dear God, thank you (in advance) for a safe drive." Almost always, whether Matthew and I, or our whole family, Matthew would lead the prayer.

One night, after some months of praying together, Matthew and I went through his usual nighttime routine. He put on his pajamas, brushed his teeth, and climbed into bed under his blankets. I knelt by the side of the bed so we could pray together. As was the case at the time, unless Matthew was really tired, he said the prayer. That night he decided to play a joke. I bowed my head and silently waited for him to pray.

"Dear God," and he paused, "thank you for a safe drive." Then he began to laugh hysterically. I thought he must have been tired from the day.

"Let's try again Matthew," my intent was to be supportive.

"Dear God," and he paused, "thank you forrrr....a safe drive." He broke out in hysteria again. This time I realized he was playing a practical joke.

As Matthew was given more opportunities to pray, such as at dinnertime or during our weekly devotionals, he did so appropriately and without prompting or modeling from me or Sonya. He always prayed, "Dear God, thank you for," something. But the something was always suitable to the situation. I had previously wondered if we would ever see this type of forward movement.

EMPOWERED BY RELATIONSHIPS

I NO LONGER battled thoughts of our family being forgotten by God. I was confident we never would be. Sonya and I had our eyes set much more on how to better understand what God had planned for us and to be available to help others. We had witnessed what God could do in our life and the lives of others, and we looked forward to seeing Him do more. Life was not perfect, and we had plenty of autism-related concerns, but we had a new faith with which to face them.

Sonya cultivated her knack for identifying resources useful to Matthew, our family, and other families with special-needs children. Having sought information and help from private and public sources for years, she knew much about state and local organizations that provided instruction, assistance, and in some cases relief to families. She began working as a trainer for an organization that educated families on the laws pertaining to public education and healthcare as it relates to children with disabilities. Sonya was good at this, and it gave her the opportunity to take steps toward the professional work she had done prior to the birth of our children. While our journey with autism brought uncounted dark days, at this juncture, Sonya discovered a place of personal fulfillment and joy in her camaraderie with other mothers determined to fight for their children, their own well-being, and the well-being of others.

Sonya and I developed meaningful friendships with some couples who had children on the spectrum, and others who did not. We found the friendships with other parents who had special-needs children to be a particularly special treasure because these people were the direct answer to our prayers. During some of our hardest times, we prayed for friendships in which we could mutually support one another. We needed to communicate freely about the nuances of living life with an autistic child, which were beyond words. With these fellow travelers, we never felt like it was not OK to talk about our experience. Often discourse about autism with persons not living the same life could be overwhelming. With these couples, for whom we had great affection, we did not have to explain life with autism, it just *was*. We longed to see them, and when parting, hated to say goodbye.

By this period of our life, family members were closer to understanding our special-needs way of life. They had also gotten to know Matthew a bit better. We did not live near the majority of our relatives, which for a long time made it hard for them to see Matthew as more than a "regular kid" with a couple of quirks. However, everyone, from my siblings, nieces and nephews, to Sonya's grandmother was there for us. They did not always apprehend or agree with our decision-making in regard to Matthew, but they had come to accept, in certain respects, our family *was* different; and they were behind us.

Sonya and I had also grown sympathetic to their need for time to make sense of the metamorphosis they observed us going through (without being able to see the details of our daily life). Specifically with regard to our parents, we were in a better place to grasp the reality that, while we had suffered over the years in relation to autism, because they loved us, and Matthew, they also grieved. Coming to a point where we were able to be more outward-focused in our perspective was good.

FAMILY WORSHIP

Love the Lord your God with all your heart and with all your soul and with all your strength. These commandments that I give you today are to be on your hearts. Impress them on your children. Talk about them when you sit at home and when you walk along the road, when you lie down and when you get up.
- Deuteronomy 6:5-8
(NIV)

OUR FAMILY HAD been doing devotionals at home on Sundays for about nine months. We were seeking a church community suitable for our entire family, and stepping away from one's long-time church home is not something we would recommend lightly. Yet we were open to what God might be teaching us through our current situation. If Sonya and I believed we played the most important role in Matthew and Jaida's academic education (and we did believe this), then we took even more seriously the call, as parents, to teach them the way of God as best we could. Therefore, Sunday meetings with a large congregation in a big church building or not, we taught them.

The implications of worshipping at home on Sundays with Matthew and Jaida were more impacting on my life than I anticipated. Sonya and I decided we would follow the pattern of worship we had learned at church over the years. This included praying together, singing, teaching a child-appropriate lesson for Matthew and Jaida, and some type of children's craft emphasizing the lesson. We also selected a memory Bible verse that we could discuss and apply over the course of the upcoming week. After volunteering to teach children's classes for so many years, we were confident that we could adequately present the gospel to our children in a way that was clear and appealing to them. However, what we did not know we lacked those many years of teaching at church, was actually going home with the children we taught and shepherding their hearts twenty-four seven. We found this to be the real lesson.

Jaida comprehended more of our devotionals than did Matthew, but they both loved and looked forward to them. They routinely requested Bible lessons throughout the week. Jaida asking, "Dad, are we going to have our Bible lesson today?" and Matthew requesting, "Bible lesson please." At other times, Matthew would come and lean very close to my face and simply say, "Let's pray. Let's pray." As much as possible, Sonya and I tried to inspire them about the greatness of God, and cultivate in them a heart of gratitude through such times and talking to them about the God who made all things. The more we taught our children biblical principles every day of the week, and strove to model who God calls us to be, the more responsible I felt to do it well.

I was amazed by God's hand, exhibited in Matthew and Jaida's natural inclination to believe in Him. It was truly a view of God's work up-close. Jaida asked honest and sincere questions I had not heard since I was a boy, such as "Why can't I see what God looks like?" or "God lives in heaven, right?" and then look to me to expound on what heaven is like. She did not require a long, complex answer, rather a direct and truthful one. I could not dismiss Jaida by spouting off scripture or giving her an Old Testament proverb. I had to stop and be mindful of her inquiry before responding. She expected no fluff answers - and to provide them required that I be perfectly clear on what I believed about things I had not stopped to think about in quite some time. In addition, if we were not well prepared for a Sunday lesson one week, Matthew and Jaida noticed.

Striving to pass on our faith to our young autistic son required prayer, because as always, there were things that we did not understand. During our Sunday worship, Matthew could become over-excited and fidgety as a result of our singing, and so, there were some Sundays when we did not sing. It was not that he did not enjoy it, but it was too much for him to process while still remaining calm. On another weekend, he might be fine and even lead us in a song. He always enjoyed the introductory game we played, and the crafts we made. At times he really enjoyed reading from his children's Bible.

Since Matthew's comprehension was not on the same level as his younger sister's, Sonya and I had to pray for understanding in order to know what (and in what way) biblical principles might resonate most with him. Matthew was not going to conceptualize (yet), that Jesus was sent to earth to save humanity. He saw things literally. He needed to touch something to know what it was really like. And he needed and enjoyed lots and lots of repetition. We kept lessons simple. We let him cut, glue, and assemble crafts from construction paper, yarn, and other materials. And we were fine with playing the same introductory game every week, using a different theme.

Our goal to join a congregation of believers was unchanged. Our circle of friends was not closed. Nonetheless, worshipping at home in the meantime nudged us to keep our faith front and center in our home. We were aware that at such young ages, Matthew and Jaida were still influenced more by us, than a society that might not be as eager for God as we were. We were clear that as they built their own relationships when older, there was at least a possibility that they would not be as inclined to believe. However, while they were at this stage of their lives, Sonya and I relished planting seeds of faith in their hearts that God would make grow over time. It was a bright and joyful time for us.

Chapter Twelve

LESSONS LEARNED

I COULD NOT sum up all we had learned, or been through with Matthew over the course of seven (going on eight) years, but I expected much more lay ahead for our family than trailed. We had yet to encounter things such as the impact of hormones on adolescent behavior, or trying to shepherd his typically developing teenage sibling through feelings of neglect while her more dependent brother got the lion share of her parent's attention. Nor had we reached the point of having to face decisions as hard as whether or not our adult child with a disability would have to live with us for the rest of his life, or, even worse in my mind, move from our home to live in an assisted care facility. We had not lived out the half of it; and we knew it.

Nevertheless, we drew on the principles we had learned through experience to steer through each new test, and in the middle of it all, we tried to have fun whenever possible. As a father and husband, I felt I had varying degrees of success and failure in helping our family life be its best, but regardless of how I interpreted things to be going at any given point in time, our run with autism to date led me to consistently view the following principles as some of the most important:

I AM NOT MY CHILD'S PROGRESS

I BATTLED WITH this for so long, I did not easily shake it. As a parent of a special needs child, I lived with a false sense of failure. I easily was caught in a trap of using Matthew's developmental progress as a measurement of how I was doing as a parent, rather than assessing how I loved, influenced, and supported Matthew.

Often, I thought if Matthew said more words and used more sentences, then I was succeeding. Or, if he were not progressing academically or potty-trained by a certain age, then I must be failing. My wife always seemed to be aware we needed to have a balanced perspective—simply by stopping to ask if we were doing the best we could for our son with our time, resources, and wisdom.

Conversely, I sometimes experienced a misplaced sense of success if Matthew did well according to a standard we, or someone else, set; potentially, this could have led me to push my son and myself in such a way that was unhealthy. Matthew needed unconditional, unwavering love and guidance. My perspective was burdensome and unfair, but, more than anything else, just was not true.

IT'S IMPORTANT TO COUNT MY BLESSINGS

ONCE, IN THE middle of the week, when Matthew was about six years old, I was to pick him up from school. Sonya and I rotated days. I had arrived at Matthew's school about thirty minutes early, which was rare. Since it was too hot to stand outside underneath the direct rays of the Georgia sun, I remained seated in my car with a book. From the parking lot, I had a clear view of the door Matthew entered in the morning and exited in the afternoon.

While I waited and read in the air-conditioning, I periodically lifted my eyes from the pages of my book to Matthew's class door in anticipation of seeing him come through it and dart away from his teachers, as he did most days. At one point as I glanced up, four young men came out of the building, walking in the general direction of where I was seated. At first impression, they appeared to be a group of teenage friends walking along laughing and talking, and I thought little of it. However as the group drew nearer, I realized three of the four youths were wearing padding on their chest that looked something like the protective gear worn by a baseball catcher; and also covered their abdominal areas and arms. As I looked, I saw one young man was flanked and guided by the others.

The youth who was being chaperoned appeared to have severe mental and physical challenges, and I could not discern his age, except to say he was a teenager. His head tilted slightly toward his left shoulder, and he had a smile on his face that seemed to indicate he was happy and that he was comfortable with the people who were attending to him. His stride was slow and he moved with a slight limp. Since his aids wore protective pads, I assumed he was capable of hurting them and himself, though by his innocent appearance I could not imagine he would do so intentionally.

On any given day, when taking Matthew to and from school, Sonya and I saw children whose limitations were more severe than his. However, for some reason, watching this boy on that day caused me to pause. I pondered what life must be like for his parents. I wondered about their hope for the future—after more than ten or fifteen years raising a child with a severe disability. I wondered what his mother felt when the boy got frustrated, upset, or out of control. As these speculative thoughts ran through my mind, I was reminded how good we had it with Matthew. Not just because he had less challenges than someone else, but because he was our child.

As Matthew approached the age of seven, he was far from

where he had started, but he had a long way to go before adversity would not be the norm. We still had days when we went up to his playroom to find him there mouthing on anything he could fit past his teeth. His self-soothing habits, such as non-stop humming, were slowing down, but they were far from gone. Raising him was not a piece of cake, yet Sonya and I shuddered at the thought of our life without him.

This did not mean I did not experience my fair share of temptation as I watched parents of typically developing children going about their lives without, what appeared to me, to be a care in the world. It did mean my relationship with my son, as well as my better judgment, told me if I entertained thoughts of who Matthew *"could be"* or *"would be"* for longer than a moment, I would miss the awesome little boy standing before me. No matter how cliché it may seem, counting my blessings is *really* important. Whenever I got away from this principle, trouble followed.

MY SON IS A GIFT FROM GOD, TO ME

FEW THINGS CAN compare to Matthew looking up at me and my wife with a smile that is the result of feeling really proud about something he has accomplished. One night after dinner, he and our four-year-old daughter Jaida were sitting at the dining room table experimenting with construction paper, markers, scissors, and glue. Matthew was intently drawing, and I was thankful he was sitting still. At some point, curiosity had me look over his shoulder to see what he was creating. The drawing looked like a man in astronaut gear. An exceptionally detailed representation that I thought was a remarkable drawing for him.

Without disturbing Matthew or Jaida, I hurried to tell Sonya to come take a look at Matthew's drawing. From the hall, together we peeked over his shoulder. "I think that's a fantastic drawing," I whispered to Sonya. "Yes," she agreed. After a few seconds, Matthew sensed our presence and, with a gigantic smile, he turned his head looking back and forth from us to his drawing. "Robot," he said, "Robot." Clearly, Matthew felt great about what he had drawn, as well as the experience of doing it.

There were few times when I had seen Matthew appear so confident. He knew he had done something well, and I had never seen him that way before. There had been times when Matthew enjoyed an activity so much he could not contain his exhilaration, but this moment was different. He was filled with a sense of accomplishment. I had never seen this expression reflected so vividly on his face and I felt his elation in every part of myself. I had recalled in my thoughts many times that Matthew was a gift of God, but through times such as this, I experienced it.

LOVE, LOVE, AND LOVE SOME MORE

ONE MORNING AFTER helping Sonya and Matthew out the door for their day, I sat down to my daily personal Bible study without a specific book, chapter, and verse in mind. Sometimes, this was the case, but often was not. Usually, in response to something weighing heavily on my mind and on my heart for a number of days, I had already earmarked what I would read.

I prayed and opened the Bible to the book of First Corinthians to look at one of the most well-known verses on love, chapter thirteen, verse eight. I wish I could say I felt the Spirit move me in a powerful way to turn to that verse, but I could not. I just happened to turn to the page after I prayed, and when I glanced at the heading of the chapter I figured meditating on the attributes of love could do me nothing but good.

"Love never fails," were the first three words of the verse. I could not count the number of times I had read or spoken this phrase throughout my years as a Christian. I had always interpreted the words to mean the act of loving always produced successful results. I thought of love as a verb, and as one of the most powerful forces in the world, accomplishing great feats despite any odds. In my mind it was similar to the nonviolent resistance to social injustice practiced by Mahatma Gandhi and Dr. Martin Luther King Jr., or Jesus Christ.

Through deeper study I saw there was some validity to how I thought about the Bible's teaching on this subject, but realized my understanding of that particular verse had been incorrect. In studying it across multiple translations, I realized more accurately, the writer was actually implying love never stops, as in, gives up or quits or ceases. A good translation is found in the Amplified Bible. It expresses the verse as "Love never fails [never fades out or becomes obsolete or comes to an end]." I was relieved to know I could go forward applying it in a more accurate manner (though not on my own), and I considered how I might apply it with my wife, my daughter Jaida, and Matthew.

I meditated deeply on the meaning of the words, and it dawned on me, love is an ongoing commitment focused on others. I considered the verse in the context of nurturing Matthew. I reflected on the times I enjoyed my relationship with him the most versus the times I felt frustrated. It occurred to me the difference between experiencing one or the other was how much I was willing to love Matthew at any point in time—in spite of his challenges. If Matthew had a bathroom accident or ran away from me in a dangerous, public setting, and I allowed myself to get angry, then that became the determining factor of my experience with him. If I were patient, then I did not miss a beat in enjoying his company. I was free to just love my son; and doing so lightened the weary load that often came with autism.

GOD IS ALWAYS AT HIS WORK

DURING THE LATE 1990's, I was involved in my church's pilot community arts school in New York City. The school offered dance, theater, music, and visual arts classes for inner-city kids of all ages to come and enjoy for free after school and on Saturdays. Our goal was to provide these students with something constructive to do during their non-school hours, while allowing them to develop their talents and character. My role was to teach visual arts classes in a meaningful and enjoyable way; one of my classes was sculpture, using the medium of clay.

My goal was to teach them the nature of the material while getting them to associate their class project with a principle they could keep with them as they went about their life. The class lasted for several weeks, and, during each session, I discussed how the process of creating with clay could relate to things they might encounter outside of our class. It was not a new concept, but it was effective.

As the students worked, I asked them to pretend they were the clay and to describe how they imagined it felt at each stage of being molded. Common answers were, "Ouch, I think this would hurt," as they threw the clay; or "Yuck, I wouldn't want to get this dirty," as they stuck their hands in the mud-like slip. As the weeks went on and they saw their projects developing into objects that pleased them, I facilitated a similar discussion, again asking them to pretend they were the clay during the later stages of the process, which were glazing and firing.

Undoubtedly, when we discussed being put into a kiln, they described the firing process as the most frightening and painful:

"No way would I get in a fire that was a thousand degrees," remarked one girl.

"But what would happen to you if you didn't?" I asked, trying to prompt her to continue reasoning, "Where would that leave you?"

"You wouldn't get dry or harden," chimed in another young man.

"Why would that be a problem?" I asked, trying to draw out their thoughts.

"You could crack later on," said one boy.

"Or you wouldn't be strong," replied another.

Then we drew comparisons between the firing process and the potential challenges they might face at home and at school. I tried to help them understand the positive role difficulties could play in their life if they approached them with the right attitude, and I tried to get them to build an association between hardships and becoming the best person, they could be. I stopped short of teaching them the importance of being willingly pliable, as that was a bit too mature of a topic for sixth- and seventh-graders. However, in the ever changing and irregular nature of my own life, remembering this was of great importance.

There are some things that cannot be learned through someone else's reality, or apprehended theoretically. For more than twenty years, I understood with my head that struggle was a prerequisite to lasting spiritual growth. However, through autism I experienced firsthand the incomprehensible way in which God produces good out of affliction. His process was (and remains) hard to grasp when in the midst of it. However, in hindsight, it brought goose bumps on my arms to reflect on a situation that seemed so unbearable, and to recognize clearly that I was never alone. Furthermore, I knew that neither I, nor my family, ever would be.

Epilogue

Great crowds came to him (Jesus), bringing the lame, the blind, the crippled, the mute and many others, and laid them at his feet; and he healed them.

- Matthew 15:30

OUR FAMILY ATTENDED an outdoor fair one Saturday in May. The event was specifically for disabled children and their families. The venue was a large parking lot about the size of a football field on the campus of a local junior college. As far as I could tell, there were about a thousand people in attendance. As we exited the car and walked toward the festivities, I was glad Jaida enjoyed these outings as much as Matthew did because that meant they were fun for our entire family. On average, we attended one organized gathering every other month.

It usually took Matthew fifteen or twenty minutes to adjust to being in the midst of a crowd, but once he felt comfortable, he began to have a good time. Matthew started his fun off by throwing balls at a dunking booth. He was thrilled when he hit the target with a large blue rubber ball, which dropped a young man into a tank of water. After hitting the target four or five times in a row, I got the impression that Matthew was vicariously jumping into the water through the man. He would have loved to be falling in the water himself. Matthew also had a blast at the kid's craft tables. Jaida had fun as well.

I felt at home among so many families I knew could relate to ours. I would have been hard pressed to find an environment that provided more confirmation that my family was not alone. Maybe that was what attracted me so much to the events. The kids that were there that afternoon varied in their abilities. Some children were in wheel chairs, some were blind, and others seemed to be not so aware of all the people around them. I appreciated how happy the children appeared, regardless of their challenges. However, at some point, among all the smiles, balloons, balls and inflatable slides, I felt saddened and stunned to think how many children with disabilities there are in our society, and I thought about the implications of the numbers for those of us who are not disabled, especially Christian believers.

The Bible speaks a lot about Jesus' ministry to the sick, lame, blind, deaf, and poor. Jesus was moved to compassion when people in these conditions were in his presence. Jesus loves the disabled, and he loves children. Those who claim to follow Jesus should do likewise. We should not just tolerate persons with special needs, or volunteer for them every now and again. We should not feel sorry for them. We should love them. Love for all was an integral aspect of the life that Jesus lived.

Repeatedly I have spoken with friends who have a special-needs child (ren), and heard from them that they are experiencing a disconnect from their church community (certainly not all, but some). Because of the extra help, attention, or accommodation that they need for their child to participate, they question whether or not there is, any longer, a place for their family within the spiritual community they have been devoted to for so long.

While this is by no means a straightforward situation, because it involves human feelings and perceptions, the simple lesson for the church (both individual Christians and leaders) is to have the heart of Jesus and reach out, as he did, to those who have disabilities. I believe that if for no reason other than the sheer increase in the number of children affected by autism and other disabilities, our communities will be driven to a change or to a cure. Whichever it is, I envision compassionate Christians leading the charge.

TO THOSE WHO are Christian parents caring for a child with a disability, and tempted to give up on their relationship with God, I want to encourage you to persevere in your journey. The constant pace and sometimes duress that exists in the life of a special-needs parent, can make one feel as if the thing they need most is to rest, or as we say a lot in our home, take a break. We strongly desire a time to do nothing, and be rejuvenated. Not enough can be said about the need for respite care that many people require in order to prevent burn out in the most basic of family roles - parenthood. However more important to know, even when we are weary, is that seeking God is a help, not a hindrance.

Each individual has to decide for themselves what spiritual disciplines help them most to draw near to God, but continuing on in things such as setting aside at the least ten minutes each day to study our Bibles, or praying in the moment when overcome with anxiety or fear (or just thanking God) can bring immeasurable peace into our lives. Other things, such as listening to and singing songs that build up your faith, calling another believer to discuss spiritual matters, and even fasting (in a safe and healthy manner) can benefit us and our families in ways that are beyond measure. God sees you, He hears you, He knows your situation, and He is working on your behalf. Do not give up. Neither my child nor yours will have autism in heaven.

Acknowledgements

WRITING A BOOK is not a solo endeavor. From Autistic to Awesome: A Journey of Spiritual Growth through Life with My Special-Needs Child would not have been possible without the help and support of many people. I am grateful to so many people who have offered words of encouragement to me while I was writing. It has meant a lot to me to know that others were excited for me simply because I was working on this project. Thank you to my wife Sonya for her love and help. Thank you to my daughter Jaida, and of course to Matthew. Thank you most of all to God, who put this book on my heart and has helped me to execute it.

I am grateful to my sister Jennifer. She has listened to me time after time, as I sorted through numerous decisions and ideas related to the literary development and the logistics of the book. Her belief in my ability to complete what I set out to do kept me going on many occasions. She has encouraged me in every possible way without wavering. It has been, and is, a tremendous help to me to know that she is in my corner. I am thankful to Jennifer for reading the early copies of my manuscript and providing valuable feedback. I am also thankful to Jennifer for referring me to my copyeditor Suzanne Frey.

Suzanne worked tirelessly on From Autistic to Awesome: A Journey of Spiritual Growth through Life with My Special-Needs Child. Her feedback, research, suggestions, and advice came out of the goodness of her heart. She took a sincere interest in the book's subject matter and engaged in editing with the pure motive of helping me. She has become a friend and her assistance has been invaluable. I cannot thank Suzanne enough.

Thank you to my brothers Gerald, Thomas, John Jr., Corey, and Ronald. Thank you to my sister Teresa, my sister-in-law Mary, and my sister-in-law Candeh. Thank you also to my nephew, Quintin, who believed in me every step of the way. My family has given me resources and moral support to write this book. As I worked to write and publish the manuscript, I learned that both were necessary to bring From Autistic to Awesome: A Journey of Spiritual Growth through Life with My Special-Needs Child to fruition. This book would not have been completed without the help of my family.

I am grateful for Willie and Sandra Woodall, Corey and Kym Gude, and William and Michelle Ward. Their lives and perseverance in loving God validate the material about which I have written. They are heroes in parenting special-needs children and in caring about others. I would like to thank William and Michelle Harris for sharing in the joy that I felt about working on this type of project, and for having a sincere excitement about it.

My long-time friend Gretchen Griffin was a source of information for me as I wrote. Sometimes she edited my writing, and at other times, she engaged with me in conversation that provided just the boost I needed to go on to the next phase of the work.

My best friend Knick Johnson has been a consistent source of inspiration and advice. Knick is always a voice of reason for me and reminds me that anything is possible through creativity, faith in God, hard work, and perseverance. Knick was a major help to me in reshaping the manuscript to make it as helpful as possible to the parents, families and caregivers for whom it is intended. Knick and I, over the course of time, had many conversations about the topics in the book. This often helped me to express my thoughts in writing.

ACKNOLEDGMENTS

Thank you to Lynda Young who I believe God led me to. Lynda's willingness to point me in the right direction has helped me to complete From Autistic to Awesome: A Journey of Spiritual Growth through Life with My Special-Needs Child. Lastly, thank you to Deb Haggerty, who after reading the book, believed in the importance of its message.

CPSIA information can be obtained at www.ICGtesting.com
Printed in the USA
LVOW041042240812

295726LV00002BA/1/P